CAPTURE *the* COAST

FOURTH IN THE SERIES

FROM

THE JUNIOR LEAGUE OF TAMPA

CULINARY COLLECTION

CREATORS OF THE GASPARILLA COOKBOOK, A TASTE OF TAMPA,
TAMPA TREASURES, THE LIFE OF THE PARTY, EVERYDAY FEASTS,
AND SAVOR THE SEASONS

To purchase copies of *Capture the Coast*,
visit us online at www.jltampa.org, complete the order form in the back of this book,
or call The Junior League of Tampa at 813-254-1734.

In the sun-drenched communities of Florida's West Coast, year-round gatherings with family and friends are our way of life. The Gulf of Mexico's crystalline waters lap at our back door, and the balmy breezes of Tampa Bay warm the air, enabling us to enjoy the outdoors nearly twelve months of the year.

From Ruskin tomatoes to red snapper, and citrus to cilantro, our region is blessed with some of the freshest produce and seafood in the country. Complementing these bountiful ingredients is the unique melding of cultures we are fortunate to share—Greek in Tarpon Springs and Cuban in Ybor City, among others. This rich heritage adds wonderful depth to the flavors you find here.

The entire Junior League of Tampa Culinary Collection reflects our love of fresh ingredients, simple preparation, and outdoor living. Whether spending a day on the boat or grilling by the pool, we prefer not to waste time in the kitchen fussing over pretentious dishes. *Capture the Coast*, the fourth book in the Culinary Collection, features wonderful recipes infused with fresh Florida flavors that are perfect for casually elegant entertaining. Join us as we set a table by the water and take a culinary journey of life in Tampa Bay.

—*Capture the Coast Committee*

CAPTURE *the* COAST

THE JUNIOR LEAGUE OF TAMPA
Culinary Collection

CAPTURE *the* COAST

Volume 4 of The Junior League of Tampa Culinary Collection

The Junior League of Tampa, Inc., is an organization of women committed to promoting voluntarism, developing the potential of women, and improving communities through effective action and leadership of trained volunteers. Its purpose is exclusively educational and charitable.

Proceeds from the sale of this cookbook will be reinvested in the community through The Junior League of Tampa projects and programs.

The Junior League of Tampa, Inc.
87 Columbia Drive
Tampa, Florida 33606
813-254-1734

Copyright © 2010 by
The Junior League of Tampa, Inc.

ISBN: 978-0-9609556-6-4
Library of Congress Control Number: 2010925005

Edited, Designed, and Produced by

 Favorite Recipes® Press

An imprint of

FRP® INC

A wholly owned subsidiary of Southwestern/Great American, Inc.
P.O. Box 305142
Nashville, Tennessee 37230
1-800-358-0560

Series Concept: David Malone
Art Director: Steve Newman
Icon and Production Designer: Travis Rader
Project Editor: Tanis Westbrook

Manufactured in the United States of America
First Printing: 2010
20,000 copies

This cookbook is a collection of favorite recipes,
which are not necessarily original recipes.

SPECIAL THANKS

A cookbook is a collaboration of many people. To all those listed here, we thank you sincerely for your part in this endeavor. We have made every effort to express our gratitude to everyone who has touched this project. If we have inadvertently left out your name, please accept our sincere apologies.

To those who so graciously gave us access to their beautiful homes and locations for the photographs in this cookbook:

Carlouel Yacht Club   Margo and Gary Harrod
Ybor City State Museum   Carolyn and Keith Bricklemyer
Ann and James Turner III   City of Tarpon Springs
Cherry and Ron Clark, Jordan Farms

To the businesses that allowed us access to props for the photographs in this cookbook:

Alvin Magnon Jewelers
Botanica International Design Studio
Connie Duglin Specialty Linen
Magnolia Furnishings, Gifts and Objects of Charm
Occasions

To our designers and photographer for the photographs in this cookbook:

COOKBOOK PHOTOGRAPHY— © Robert Adamo

FOOD STYLIST—Kristie Salzer

FLORIST—Botanica International Design Studio, Ian Prosser, designer

THE JUNIOR LEAGUE OF TAMPA CULINARY COLLECTION LOGO—
MarketingDirection.com, Christy Atlas-Vogel

COOKBOOK DEVELOPMENT COMMITTEE

CHAIRMAN—Laurie Ann Burton

ASSISTANT CHAIRMAN—Ashley Carl

COPYWRITING/EDITING—Patricia Brawley, Jodi Rivera

PHOTOGRAPHY COORDINATORS—Veronica Kruchten, Stacey Waters

RECIPE SELECTION COORDINATORS—Jenn Hunt, Carolyn Piper, Lisl Unterholzner, Leah Wooten

Jennifer L. Johnson, President 2008–2009

Jen Carlstedt, President 2009–2010

Betsy Graham, President 2010–2011

COVER PHOTO SPONSORS

FRONT COVER IMAGE—Mary Lee Nunnally Farrior
BACK COVER IMAGE—Laura Mickler Bentley

LEADING SPONSORS

Campbell and Don Burton
Terrie Dodson and Mark Caldevilla
Betsy and Drew Graham

CHAPTER PHOTO SPONSORS

Chapter One—TOAST OF THE COAST
This photograph was generously underwritten by Ashley and Eric Carl.

Chapter Two—REFRESHERS
This photograph was generously underwritten by The Junior League of Tampa Presidents:
Jennifer L. Johnson (2008–09), Jen Carlstedt (2009–10), Betsy Graham (2010–11), and
Laura Hobby (2011–12).

Chapter Three—SIDES & SUCH
This photograph was generously underwritten by The Junior League of Tampa Sustainer Presidents:
Patty Ayala (2003–04), Sally Hardee (2004–05), Helen Brown (2005–06), Nadyne Hines
(2006–07), Julie Lux (2007–08), Patti Henderson Cowart (2008–09), Rosann Martin Creed
(2009–10), and Liz Reynolds (2010–11).

Chapter Four—MAIN ATTRACTIONS
This photograph was generously underwritten by the 2009–10 Provisional Class and Committee.

Chapter Five—TEMPTATIONS
This photograph was generously underwritten by the Development Chairs of the Culinary
Collection: Danielle Andres Welsh, Chair-The Life of the Party, Terrie Dodson, Chair-
EveryDay Feasts, Taylour Smedley Shimkus, Chair-Savor the Seasons, and Laurie Ann
Burton, Chair-Capture the Coast.

MENU PHOTO SPONSORS

PIRATE'S TREASURE
This photograph was generously underwritten by Lisa Andrews, Christy Atlas-Vogel, Danelle Barksdale, Barrie Buenaventura, Renee Dabbs, Katherine Frazier, Lisa Gabler, Suzanne Gabler, Michelle Hogan, Leigh Kaney, Trish Lane, Mindy Murphy, Joellyn Rocha, Carla Saavedra, Michelle Schofner, and Susan Thompson.

ON THE SETIMA
This photograph was generously underwritten by Louise Ferguson and Stella Thayer.

THRILL OF THE GRILL
This photograph was generously underwritten by Pam and Brett Divers.

CAPTAIN'S TABLE
This photograph was generously underwritten by Barbara Harvey Ryals (The Junior League of Tampa President, 1999–2000) and Nancy Harvey Mynard (The Junior League of Tampa President, 2002–2003).

BOAT & TOTE
This photograph was generously underwritten by June S. Annis.

IT'S GREEK TO ME
This photograph was generously underwritten by Horizon Bay at Hyde Park.

FROM THE FIELDS
This photograph was generously underwritten by Adajean Lott Samson.

WOMEN BUILDING BETTER COMMUNITIES

The Junior League of Tampa cookbooks have always served as a legacy, an investment of time and tradition, handed from one generation to another, from our community to yours. But more than that, The Junior League of Tampa cookbooks are an investment in the foundation of our community.

Since 1926, the volunteers in our organization have shared their time, talents, and treasures with the Tampa community. Here is a glimpse of some of the projects and organizations that we have been proud to support through volunteer hours and money raised through fund-raisers, including the sale of our cookbooks.

Academy Prep Center of Tampa
Alpha House of Tampa
America's Second Harvest & Kids Cafe/ Food 4 Kids Project
Baby Bungalow, An Early Childhood Resource and Support Center
Child Abuse Task Force
Children's Cancer Center
Children's Literacy Project
Connected by 25
Drug Abuse Comprehensive Coordinating Office (DACCO)
Fun Book/Fun Cart and Puppet Troupe for Hospitalized Children
Glazer Children's Museum and Kid City
Hillsborough Kids Inc./Kids Connect Special Needs Adoption Events
H. Lee Moffitt Hospital & Cancer Research Institute
Hope Preparatory Academy
Kids in the Kitchen Project
Love Bundles Project
MacDonald Training Center
Mary Lee's House
Metropolitan Ministries Day Care Center
Minority Youth Leadership Program for Girls
MORE HEALTH, A Health Education and Injury Prevention Program
PACE Center for Girls
Reading is Fundamental (RIF)
SERVE—Volunteers in Education
Tampa Bay Performing Arts Center
Tampa General Sunshine House/ Ronald McDonald House
The Children's Home
The Spring of Tampa Bay, A Domestic Violence Shelter

Contents

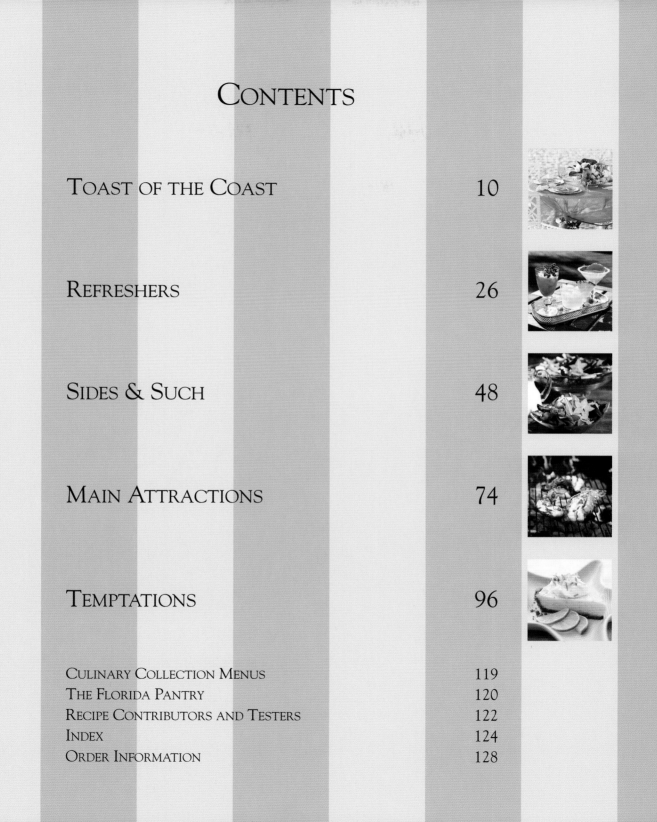

CAPTURE THE COAST

TOAST OF THE COAST

CULINARY COLLECTION

PIRATE'S TREASURE

MENU

THE LUCKY SEVEN COCKTAILS

SPANAKOPITA PHYLLO CUPS

CRAB CAKES WITH SPICY MUSTARD

DILL DIP WITH CRUDITÉS

HAMWICH

TENDERLOIN SLIDERS WITH
ROASTED GARLIC LIME SAUCE

BERN'S CARROT CAKE BROWNIES WITH
TOASTED PECAN FROSTING

Bayshore Boulevard is Tampa's landmark street. Lined with stately historic homes, this linear park and roadway curves along Hillsborough Bay, connecting South Tampa and Historic Hyde Park to Channelside Drive and the downtown district. Every day parents strolling their children, cross country teams, inline skaters, and bikers enjoy the view while taking advantage of the world's longest continuous sidewalk, spanning about four and a half miles. On a clear day you can see rowers in their sculls, sailboats, fishing boats, and cruise liners in the distance. Across the Bay, hints of smoke stacks remind you that Tampa is a busy, industrial port city.

Though spectacular any time of year, Bayshore Boulevard really comes to life in January during the Gasparilla invasion. In a more than century-old tradition, locals dress in costume, many as unrecognizable pirates, and invade the city. Early in the morning, the pirates' mighty vessel, the José Gaspar, enters Hillsborough Bay, joined by revelers forming a flotilla hundreds strong. Once the mayor surrenders the keys to the City, the entire community celebrates what's been referred to as Tampa's Mardi Gras, with a festive parade down Bayshore Boulevard led by the pirates and krewes. Many of the homes along Bayshore host fabulous cocktail parties to toast the parade, creating a festive backdrop for this memorable, annual event.

The Junior League of Tampa's cookbooks have long celebrated the flavors of our pirate festival. In the pages of our past cookbooks, you will find recipes for Pirate's Milk Punch and Cuban sandwiches—staples of any Gasparilla party.

ON THE SETIMA

A vivid blend of lively cultural influences lies at the heart of Tampa. Along the brick streets of Tampa's historic Ybor City, you'll find a unique melding of ethnic backgrounds. Known as Tampa's Latin Quarter, Ybor City was once home to Cubans, Spaniards, and Italians, who brought their traditions to the area. Tampa's history holds other lasting influences—flavors passed through generations of families. Today we continue to enjoy these recipes, many of which were featured prominently in The Junior League of Tampa's original cookbook, *The Gasparilla Cookbook*, published in 1961.

Formerly known as the "Cigar Capital of the World," Ybor City once produced more quality cigars than Havana. While the cigar factories served as the economic engine of Ybor City, social clubs formed by distinct immigrant groups became central to community support and growth. Many of the buildings that housed clubs, such as El Centro Español, the Italian Club, and Circulo Cubano have

MENU

STRAWBERRY-CITRUS SANGRIA

COLUMBIA RESTAURANT'S "1905" SALAD

MUSSELS SPANISH STYLE

PICADILLO WRAPPED IN PASTRY

FRIJOLES NEGROS WITH RICE

COLUMBIA RESTAURANT'S FLAN

been restored to their original architectural glory and are still used today.

Recognized by the Trust for Historic Preservation as a Landmark Historic District, Ybor City successfully blends its preserved architecture with modern-day functionality. Walk through this popular entertainment district today, and you're sure to experience the sights, smells, and sounds of old Ybor: fresh-roasted coffee beans for Café Con Leche, palm fronds baked upon loaves of toasty Cuban bread, and lively music in the streets. The famous Columbia Restaurant, whose doors opened in 1905, also continues to thrive, offering diners exceptional Cuban and Spanish food, nightly performances by flamenco dancers in its Latin ballroom, and, of course, cigars. Many more exciting restaurants, concert halls, and bars fill rehabilitated cigar factories lining La Setima (7th Avenue) and the surrounding streets, helping to keep this unique neighborhood and its traditions alive and well.

THRILL OF THE GRILL

MENU

FRESH LIME JUICE MARGARITA

LAYERED SHRIMP DIP

TRIO OF KEBABS—MOJO BEEF KEBABS,
SPICE-RUBBED SHRIMP KEBABS,
CHICKEN KEBABS

FLORIDA LOBSTER WITH
LEMON BASIL BUTTER

SUMMER VEGETABLES OVER COUSCOUS

FLORIDA KEY LIME PIE WITH
GINGERSNAP CRUST

On the Florida Gulf Coast, grilling takes on many personalities, from a big event, game-day ritual, or competitive cook-off, to a weeknight meal, child's birthday party, or impromptu date night. Whatever the occasion, cooking out makes the perfect recipe for good food and a good time.

In the Tampa Bay area, we've elevated the barbecue to a new level of gourmet preparation no longer limited to charcoal. A host of wood selections like apple, hickory, or pecan can impart great flavor to whatever you are preparing, and different cookers add uniqueness as well. From smokers to ceramic cookers to the faithful charcoal grill, each backyard grillsmith has his preferred method. We also love to look beyond the simple fare of burgers or steak, taking full advantage of local ingredients. Grilled fresh veggies, seafood, and even fruit have immense flavor when cooked over an open flame.

The season from October to May brings Tampa's best outdoor entertaining opportunities, when we're fortunate to be eating on our patios while others are curled up by the fireplace. From poolside tranquility to a golf course view, the Gulf Coast offers countless backyard settings to enjoy meals from the grill.

CAPTAIN'S TABLE

MENU
CHAMPAGNE LIME COOLER
STONE CRAB CLAWS WITH SPICY MUSTARD SAUCE
OYSTERCATCHERS' GULF SNAPPER PASSION FRUIT CEVICHE
WEEKNIGHT SURF AND TURF
SWEET ONION SOUFFLÉ
CHOCOLATE TART

It may come as a surprise to visitors that Tampa is recognized as much for extraordinary steak houses as for seafood restaurants. The oldest cattle-raising state with the longest saltwater shoreline in the contiguous forty-eight states, Florida has strong roots in both land and sea—each with a host of fresh, high-quality culinary possibilities.

The year-round availability of fresh seafood spoils many Tampa natives. Whether we're savoring a meal of scallops during the summer scalloping season, enjoying the buttery flavor of lobsters grabbed on a quick trip to the Florida Keys, or hosting a seafood feast of stone crab claws and recently caught snapper, choices abound. The day's fresh catch often makes it to our tables within hours of being caught. Inshore anglers land redfish, snook, and seatrout, while deeper waters are home to grouper, snapper, and pompano. And let's not forget shrimp, with its limitless preparation options. Even if you're not the one catching the fish—although that can be a particular treat—we're sure you'll be hooked on our local bounty.

While a pleasure on its own, seafood can be simply sublime when paired with fresh beef from a Florida ranch. The largest cattle-producer east of the Mississippi, our state provides an ideal setting for tender, mouthwatering steaks. It stands to reason that Tampa is home to many world-renowned steakhouses—most notably Bern's—where diners often wait months for a reservation.

You really can't go wrong with top-quality seafood or steaks—and the combination is bound to be a crowd-pleaser.

BOAT & TOTE

MENU

ICED GINGER TEA

MELON, CUCUMBER AND
TOMATO SALAD

MEDITERRANEAN ORZO SALAD

WRIGHT'S DILL POTATO SALAD

ANTIPASTI SANDWICH

TRIPLE CHOCOLATE COOKIES

LEMON-LIME SHORTBREAD

An outdoor meal offers the perfect opportunity to take in Tampa's impressive natural beauty—from stunning sunsets to lush oak canopies and crystalline waters. Perhaps not as well known to visitors are our variety of waterways, like the Hillsborough River that winds through downtown Tampa, hundreds of lakes, and ten bays, providing plenty of idyllic dining spots. There are a few things to keep in mind, though, when planning your relaxing meal alfresco. An afternoon shower comes more often than not in the summer months, and it may be best to avoid the peak of humidity. Other than that, it's pretty simple, as most things in Tampa tend to be.

Popular outdoor excursions in Tampa Bay feature protected preserves and scenic residential areas. In Pinellas County, the historic Fort De Soto Park spans more than one thousand acres and five interconnected islands, with access to both Tampa Bay and the pristine waters of the Gulf of Mexico. Take a lunch on a day trip to see the battery and white sand beaches, or prepare a fun dinner for an overnight campout. With over 3,700 acres, the Weedon Island Preserve is another nearby gem. Known for its bird-watching, this park has abundant nature trails and even an observation tower. You can feed a group or have a quick bite to eat at the pavilion or one of the picnic spots. For a different mood, the exquisite homes along Bayshore Boulevard and Davis Islands offer the perfect backdrop for cocktails and hors d'oeuvres on a sunset cruise.

Our picturesque, waterfront areas welcome a relaxing picnic or a tranquil, aquatic outing. Take a satisfying snack on a kayak or canoe exploration, or make a full spread of food for a breezier motor boat adventure. You really can't go wrong when planning a waterside meal. Pick a place, pack your spread, grab some friends, and enjoy!

IT'S GREEK TO ME

MENU

SHRIMP SAGANAKI

BACON-WRAPPED STUFFED DATES

PASTITSIO

CHICK-PEA AND SPINACH SALAD

TAMPA'S BAKLAVA

GREEK HONEY CAKES

Located about thirty miles northwest of Tampa, Tarpon Springs boasts the largest population of Greek-Americans of any city in the U.S. The climate, which is similar to the Mediterranean, attracted the original Greek immigrants, who arrived during the 1880s to work as divers in the area's thriving sponge-harvesting industry. Tarpon Springs is still recognized as "the sponge capital of the world." Most of the sponge docks and warehouses are now tourist attractions, and the area continues to offer visitors some of the most authentic Greek food outside of Greece.

Tarpon Springs also hosts a famous Greek Orthodox Epiphany celebration. This unique annual event draws Greek-Americans from around the world and culminates with the ceremonial Epiphany dive for the cross. As a rite-of-passage, boys ages sixteen to eighteen years old dive into Spring Bayou for the cherished cross, and the lucky retriever is considered blessed for a full year. Following the dive, families come together to feast in celebration of one of the most holy days of the year.

Appetizing and healthy, Greek cuisine features many of the same fresh ingredients that thrive on the Gulf Coast—citrus, herbs, fish, shrimp, and honey. In the Greek culture, a meal is as much about flavor as it is about sharing community, family, and friendship—similar to our Florida way of life. So enjoy the tastes of the Mediterranean, and don't forget: Opa!

FROM THE FIELDS

The West Coast of Florida is a place of abundance—sunshine, beautiful scenery, seafood, and particularly fresh produce. Many fruits, vegetables, and herbs are grown around Tampa, where our rich soil makes for a robust farming environment and our moderate temperatures allow for a year-round growing season. These ripe conditions create big flavors, which can be enjoyed in a variety of ways. Take your pick at local strawberry farms, visit plentiful roadside stands, or browse one of the many outdoor farmers' markets.

Just outside of Tampa, Plant City is known as the "Winter Strawberry Capital of the World," producing most of the winter strawberries in the U.S. To celebrate the annual harvest, Plant City hosts its famous Strawberry Festival, which dates back to 1930 and attracts visitors from across the country. The Tampa area is also home to local farming communities like Ruskin, formerly known as "America's Salad Bowl" for its mouth-watering tomatoes feted each year at the Ruskin Tomato Festival. Tampa and its surrounding areas boast more than 2,600 farms, producing an assortment of crops such as squash, beans, eggplant, and peppers, along with herbs like rosemary, cilantro, and mint.

Perhaps the most famous local crop is our prized Florida citrus. The juicy taste of a Florida orange, grapefruit, or Key lime is an almost transcendental experience. We're proud of our fresh produce; it's a fun, colorful, and easy feature in our meals, and it's just one more reason we love life in Tampa Bay.

MENU

MINT TEA LEMONADE

MINI TOMATO ROUND

LEMON-HERB ROASTED CHICKEN

ASPARAGUS AND CITRUS SALAD

GRILLED CORN WITH
HERBED COMPOUND BUTTER

STRAWBERRY SHORTCAKE WITH
SWEET CREAM BISCUITS

REFRESHERS

THE LUCKY SEVEN COCKTAILS

One recipe, seven variations, all making use of one of our favorite flavors—mint.
This simple syrup sweetens drinks more easily than granulated sugar, and the kiss of mint is
a wonderful complement to so many flavors.

MINT SIMPLE SYRUP

2 cups sugar   1/4 teaspoon fresh lemon juice
1 cup water   1 cup whole mint leaves

Mix the sugar, water, lemon juice and mint in a saucepan. Bring to a boil over medium heat, stirring constantly. Reduce the heat. Simmer for 1 minute or until the sugar is dissolved. Remove from the heat to cool. Strain into a small pitcher, discarding the mint leaves.

Yield: about 2 cups

FRESH LIME JUICE MARGARITA

1 1/2 cups silver (blanco) tequila   6 tablespoons Cointreau
1 1/2 cups fresh lime juice   Lime wedges
1/2 cup plus 2 tablespoons   Coarse kosher salt
Mint Simple Syrup   Mint leaves

Combine the tequila, lime juice, Mint Simple Syrup and liqueur in a pitcher and mix well. Chill for several hours. Moisten the rim of each margarita glass with a lime wedge and then dip in kosher salt. Pour the margarita over ice in the prepared glasses and garnish with mint and additional lime wedges on cocktail skewers.

Yield: 8 servings

MINT TEA LEMONADE

7 cups water	1 (16-ounce) can frozen lemonade
8 (single-serving) bags green tea	concentrate, thawed
7 cups water	3/4 cup Mint Simple Syrup

Bring 7 cups water to a boil in a saucepan. Add the tea bags and steep for 2 to 3 minutes. Discard the tea bags. Cool the tea to room temperature. Combine 7 cups water and the lemonade concentrate in a pitcher and mix well. Add the cool tea and Mint Simple Syrup and mix well. Chill before serving. Pour over ice in glasses to serve.

Yield: 16 servings

CITRUS SIPPER WITH FRESH MINT

1 1/2 cups fresh lemon juice	2 cups Mint Simple Syrup
1 cup fresh lime juice	3 cups lemon-flavored sparkling
1 cup fresh orange juice	water, chilled

Combine the lemon juice, lime juice, orange juice and Mint Simple Syrup in a large pitcher and mix well. Chill until serving time. Stir in the sparkling water just before serving. For an alcoholic variation, add 2 1/2 cups vodka.

Yield: 8 servings

PINEAPPLE MOJITO PITCHER

3/4 cup light rum	1/3 cup Triple Sec or other
1 (6-ounce) can pineapple juice	orange liqueur
1/3 cup fresh lime juice	2 cups club soda
1/3 cup Mint Simple Syrup	Mint leaves

Combine the rum, pineapple juice, lime juice, Mint Simple Syrup, liqueur and club soda in a large pitcher and mix well. Bruise some mint leaves with the back of a knife and add to the pitcher. Serve over ice in glasses. Garnish with additional mint leaves.

Yield: 4 servings

PRINCESS PUNCH

4 cups seedless watermelon chunks
2 cups lemonade
6 tablespoons Mint Simple Syrup
2 tablespoons fresh lemon juice
3 cups club soda, chilled

Process the watermelon and lemonade in a blender on low until smooth. Add the Mint Simple Syrup and lemon juice and blend briefly. Pour through a strainer into a pitcher, pressing on the solids to extract as much of the juice as possible. You should have about 4 cups of liquid. Chill before serving. Stir in the club soda just before serving. For *Queen's Punch*, reduce the club soda to $1^1/2$ cups and add $1^1/2$ cups vodka.

Yield: 8 servings

POMEGRANATE SUNSET

1 cup pomegranate juice
1 cup Mint Simple Syrup
$1/2$ cup fresh lime juice
$1^1/2$ cups vodka
1 (1-liter) bottle club soda, chilled
8 sprigs of fresh mint

Mix the pomegranate juice, Mint Simple Syrup, lime juice and vodka in a pitcher. Chill before serving. Stir just before serving. Fill each glass halfway with the juice mixture. Add club soda to fill each glass. Garnish with the mint.

Yield: 8 servings

A TASTE OF FLORIDA

2 cups grapefruit juice
$1^1/2$ cups tangerine juice
1 cup apricot nectar
1 cup Mint Simple Syrup
1 cup seltzer water or club soda
1 slice pink grapefruit, cut into quarters

Blend the grapefruit juice, tangerine juice, apricot nectar and Mint Simple Syrup in a pitcher. Pour over crushed ice in a tall pitcher. Stir in the seltzer water just before serving. Garnish with the grapefruit. For an alcoholic variation, add $1^1/2$ cups vodka.

Yield: 6 servings

CHAMPAGNE LIME COOLER

*A refreshing sipper for entertaining al fresco. For a nonalcoholic version,
substitute sparkling grape juice for the Champagne.*

1 cup lemon-lime soda
1 cup assorted berries, such as
raspberries, blueberries and
strawberries

1 (6-ounce) can frozen limeade
concentrate, thawed
1 (750-milliliter) bottle Champagne
or sparkling white wine
Mint

Combine the lemon-lime soda, berries and limeade concentrate in a pitcher and mix well.
Stir in the Champagne gradually. Garnish with mint and serve immediately.

Yield: 6 to 8 servings

MANGO-PINEAPPLE PUNCH

*A tropical tornado! To make ahead of time, blend all of the ingredients except the
lemon-lime soda. Add the lemon-lime soda just before serving.*

3/4 cup silver (blanco) tequila
1 (6-ounce) can pineapple juice
1 (5.5-ounce) can mango nectar
6 tablespoons peach schnapps or
peach liqueur

1/4 cup fresh lime juice
1 (12-ounce) can lemon-lime soda
6 pineapple slice wedges
6 maraschino cherries

Combine the tequila, pineapple juice, mango nectar, peach schnapps, lime juice and lemon-lime
soda in a pitcher and blend well. Thread a pineapple wedge and a maraschino cherry on each of six
cocktail skewers. Pour the punch into ice-filled glasses and garnish with a prepared skewer.

Yield: 6 servings

STRAWBERRY-CITRUS SANGRIA

The addition of strawberries gives this traditional Spanish beverage local character,
and the rich colors make for a beautiful presentation.

1 orange, sliced	3/4 cup orange liqueur
1 lemon, sliced	1 pint strawberries, thickly sliced
1 (750-milliliter) bottle pinot noir	6 ounces soda water, chilled
3/4 cup sugar, or more to taste	

Place the orange and lemon slices in a pitcher. Add the wine and sugar and mix well. Add the liqueur and mix well. Add the strawberries. Chill for 3 to 10 hours. Add the soda water before serving. Serve over ice in glasses.

Yield: 6 to 8 servings

ZESTY SUNDAY MORNING BLOODY MARY

Rimmed with Old Bay seasoning and garnished with a shrimp, this coastal
Bloody Mary makes any morning feel like a vacation day.

6 cups tomato juice, Clamato, vegetable juice cocktail or your favorite nonspicy Bloody Mary mix	1 tablespoon Old Bay seasoning
	10 (about) lemon or lime wedges
	6 boiled or cooked shrimp
1/4 cup horseradish	12 large stuffed green olives
1 tablespoon Worcestershire sauce	9 to 12 ounces vodka or tequila
2 teaspoons freshly ground pepper	Tabasco sauce to taste
2 teaspoons celery salt, or to taste	6 ribs celery
1/4 cup kosher salt	

Mix the tomato juice, horseradish, Worcestershire sauce, pepper and celery salt in a pitcher. Mix the kosher salt and Old Bay seasoning on a plate. Rub the glasses with a lemon wedge to moisten and then dip into the kosher salt mixture to coat. Thread a shrimp onto each of six wooden picks and attach an olive to the end of each. Fill the prepared glasses with ice. Add 1 1/2 to 2 ounces of vodka to each glass. Fill with the tomato juice mixture and add Tabasco sauce to taste. Top each with a shrimp skewer, celery rib and lemon wedge.

Yield: 6 servings

ICED GINGER TEA

If sweet tea is the Champagne of the South, then this
Iced Ginger Tea is the Dom Perignon!

8 cups water	1/4 cup honey
1/2 cup grated fresh ginger	4 (single-serving) bags green tea
1/3 cup fresh lemon juice	11/2 cups sugar

Bring the water, ginger, lemon juice and honey to a boil in a saucepan. Reduce the heat and simmer for 5 minutes. Remove from the heat. Add the tea bags. Steep for 5 minutes and then discard the tea bags. Stir in the sugar until dissolved. Let stand until cool. Pour through a strainer into a pitcher, discarding the solids. Serve over ice in glasses.

Yield: 8 servings

CAFECITO—CUBAN-STYLE COFFEE

This traditional Cuban coffee offers a jump-start, whether it's your morning cup or
an afternoon pick-up. The dark roasting of the beans imparts a distinctive flavor on Cuban-style
coffee, which can be sampled in brands like Bustello, Pilon, and Ybor City's own Café Modelo.

Espresso-ground Cuban dark roast coffee or
Colombian dark roast coffee
Cold water
1 teaspoon sugar per demitasse cup of coffee, or to taste

Fill the bottom half of a stovetop espresso maker with cold water. Place the metal filter basket onto the pot and fill with coffee, packing gently and leveling off evenly. Screw the top portion with the gasket on tightly and brew. When the top portion of the pot is about one-fourth full, pour over the sugar in a separate bowl and stir to dissolve. Continue brewing until all of the water has risen to the top and a sputtering sound is heard. Return the sweetened coffee to the top of the pot. Pour into demitasse cups and serve immediately. Mix equal parts brewed Cuban coffee with scalded milk for *Café con Leche*.

Yield: a variable amount

SHRIMP SAGANAKI

*Like many Greek seafood dishes, Shrimp Saganaki combines fresh ingredients with
simple preparation. Our recipe makes the tomato and red pepper purée separately, ahead of time
if you wish, so it comes together very quickly for a dinner party or weeknight meal.*

FRESH TOMATO AND
RED PEPPER PURÉE
2 tablespoons olive oil
1/2 cup chopped onion
1 garlic clove, chopped
3 cups chopped red bell peppers
(about 2 large)
2 cups chopped ripe tomatoes on
the vine (about 3 medium)
1/2 teaspoon kosher salt, or to taste

1 tablespoon balsamic vinegar
5 basil leaves, cut into thin strips
2 tablespoons flat-leaf parsley, chopped

SHRIMP SAGANAKI
1 1/2 pounds medium shrimp, peeled,
deveined and tails removed
1 (14-ounce) can quartered artichoke
hearts, drained
8 ounces crumbled feta cheese

For the purée, heat the olive oil in a large saucepan over medium heat. Add the onion and sauté
until soft. Add the garlic, bell peppers and tomatoes. Cover and reduce the heat to low. Cook for 10 to
12 minutes or until the vegetables are soft. Stir in the salt and balsamic vinegar. Purée in a blender or food
processor. Stir in the basil and parsley. The purée may be made up to 1 day in advance.

For the shrimp saganaki, preheat the oven to 350 degrees. Position the oven rack in the upper third
of the oven. Divide the shrimp and artichoke hearts among six to eight small shallow baking dishes or
ramekins or place in a shallow 1 1/2-quart baking dish. Top with the purée and sprinkle evenly with the
cheese. Place the small baking dishes on a baking sheet. Bake for 10 to 15 minutes or until the shrimp
turns pink. Broil for 5 minutes or until the cheese melts and is light brown and the sauce is bubbly. Serve
as an appetizer with crusty bread or as a main dish over angel hair pasta or spaghetti.

Yield: 6 to 8 servings

MUSSELS SPANISH STYLE

Mussels make a festive starter for a group meal, and this particular preparation creates a pleasant aroma. Soaking the mussels in water and flour before cooking filters out some of the saltiness and grit.

4 pounds mussels	1 cup chopped tomatoes
1/2 cup all-purpose flour	3/4 cup parsley, chopped
3/4 cup minced shallots or onion	2 cups white wine
3 tablespoons olive oil	Salt and pepper to taste
5 garlic cloves, minced	

Place the mussels in a large bowl and cover with water. Sprinkle with the flour. Soak for 30 minutes. Drain and remove the beards from the mussels. Discard any mussels that are opened or partially opened. Cook the shallots in the olive oil in a large stockpot until translucent and softened. Add the garlic and cook for 1 to 2 minutes or until fragrant. Add the tomatoes, parsley, wine, salt and pepper. Cook over medium-low heat for 5 to 10 minutes to blend the flavors. Stir in the mussels. Cook, covered, over medium heat for 8 to 10 minutes or until the shells open. Pour into a large serving bowl with all of the accumulated juices. Serve at once, discarding any unopened mussels.

Yield: 6 servings

GULF COAST OYSTERS

While Apalachicola Bay is the most famous source of Gulf oysters, oyster beds are found all along the coast, particularly where freshwater meets saltwater, discharging nutrients carried downstream. Enjoy freshly shucked oysters with a squeeze of lemon, a little cocktail sauce, and a saltine, or top with a dab of garlic butter and place the oyster on the half shell on a grill rack and grill until the edges curl and the butter is bubbly for an out-of-this-world experience.

CRAB CAKES WITH SPICY MUSTARD

The ever-popular crab cake gets a kick from this creamy mustard sauce.
Make miniature cakes for an exceptional cocktail party appetizer.

SPICY MUSTARD
1 1/2 tablespoons whole grain mustard
1/2 cup mayonnaise
1 tablespoon Dijon mustard
1 1/2 teaspoons horseradish

CRAB CAKES
2 tablespoons butter
1 1/2 tablespoons finely chopped
green onions (about 2)
1/2 cup finely chopped red bell pepper
(about 1/2 red bell pepper)
1 jalapeño chile, seeded and
finely chopped

2 tablespoons all-purpose flour
3 tablespoons heavy cream
2 egg yolks
2 tablespoons Dijon mustard
1 tablespoon chopped fresh chives
1 teaspoon cayenne pepper
1 teaspoon Old Bay seasoning
1 pound lump crab meat
Salt and black pepper to taste
1 cup all-purpose flour
3 eggs, beaten
2 cups Japanese bread crumbs (panko)
1 cup canola oil

For the spicy mustard, mix the whole grain mustard, mayonnaise, Dijon mustard and horseradish in a bowl. Prepare the day before and store in the refrigerator to allow the flavors to blend.

For the crab cakes, melt the butter in a 9-inch sauté pan over medium heat. Add the green onions, bell pepper and jalapeño chile and cook until soft. Stir in 2 tablespoons flour. Cook over medium heat for 4 to 5 minutes or until light blonde in color, stirring constantly. Stir in the cream. Remove from the heat. Combine the egg yolks, Dijon mustard, chives, cayenne pepper and Old Bay seasoning in a mixing bowl and mix well. Add the vegetable mixture a small amount at a time, stirring constantly. Fold in the crab meat. Add salt and black pepper to taste. Divide into twelve equal portions and shape into crab cakes. Dredge in 1 cup flour. Dip into the beaten eggs and then dredge in the bread crumbs. Place on a tray. Freeze for 30 minutes or up to 10 hours. Heat the canola oil in a deep frying pan to 350 degrees. Place the crab cakes carefully in the hot oil. Fry for 2 minutes or until golden brown on the bottom. Turn and fry until golden brown. Remove to paper towels to drain. Sprinkle with salt and black pepper to taste. Serve with the spicy mustard for dipping.

Yield: 6 servings

OYSTERCATCHERS' GULF SNAPPER PASSION FRUIT CEVICHE

A gorgeous view overlooking Tampa Bay and the creative cuisine of Chef Kenny Hunsberger draw locals and visitors to Oystercatchers Restaurant.

CITRUS CURED SNAPPER
1 pound fresh Gulf snapper
$3/4$ cup fresh lemon juice
$3/4$ cup fresh lime juice
$1/2$ cup fresh orange juice

PASSION FRUIT DRESSING
6 large passion fruit
$1/4$ cup olive oil
2 teaspoons grated fresh ginger
$1/2$ teaspoon chopped garlic
2 tablespoons chopped basil
$1/2$ teaspoon salt
$1/4$ teaspoon pepper

CRISP PLANTAIN CHIPS
2 green plantains
Vegetable oil
1 teaspoon salt
$1/4$ teaspoon pepper

ASSEMBLY
$1/4$ cup julienned red onion
$1/4$ cup julienned green bell pepper
$1/4$ cup julienned jicama
2 fresh guavas, cut into thin wedges
$1/4$ cup chopped toasted cashews

For the fish, cut the fish into thin bite-size pieces. Place in a nonreactive bowl. Pour the juices over the fish in a bowl. Marinate, covered, in the refrigerator for 1 to 2 hours or until the fish is opaque and can be easily pulled apart.

For the dressing, split the passion fruit into halves. Remove the seeds and discard. Scoop out the pulp from the shells and press through a fine mesh strainer into a glass measure to extract $1/2$ cup of juice. Combine the juice with the olive oil, ginger, garlic, basil, salt and pepper in a bowl and mix well. Chill, covered, for 8 to 10 hours.

For the plantain chips, split the skin of the plantains lengthwise. Peel the plantains by carefully sliding your thumb between the skin and the fruit. Cut the fruit lengthwise into thin strips. Fry in a small amount of oil in a skillet over medium heat until golden brown and crispy; drain. Sprinkle with the salt and pepper while warm. The chips may be made ahead and stored in an airtight container.

For the assembly, drain the fish, removing as much of the liquid as possible. Combine the fish, onion, bell pepper, jicama and dressing in a bowl and toss lightly. Adjust the seasonings. Arrange the guava on a serving plate. Top with the fish mixture and sprinkle with the cashews. Serve with the plantain chips.

Yield: 6 to 8 servings

SHRIMP COCKTAIL WITH TWO SAUCES

Succulent, chilled shrimp is always a crowd-pleaser. Try it with one or both sauces.

RÉMOULADE SAUCE
1 cup mayonnaise
1 hard-cooked egg, chopped
1/4 cup flat-leaf parsley, chopped
1 tablespoon chiffonade of fresh
    basil leaves
1 tablespoon fresh oregano, chopped
1 tablespoon fresh dill weed, chopped
1 tablespoon capers,
    drained and chopped
1 tablespoon minced red onion
1 teaspoon minced garlic
1 teaspoon fresh lemon juice
1 teaspoon horseradish, or more to taste
1/2 teaspoon Worcestershire sauce

ROASTED GARLIC
COCKTAIL SAUCE
1 1/4 cups ketchup
2 tablespoons horseradish
2 tablespoons chopped or mashed
    Roasted Garlic (page 43)
2 teaspoons fresh lemon juice
1/2 teaspoon Worcestershire sauce

STEAMED SHRIMP
2 teaspoons adobo seasoning or
    garlic powder
1 teaspoon salt
1/2 teaspoon pepper
1 bay leaf
3 to 5 pounds large Gulf shrimp,
    peeled and deveined

For the rémoulade sauce, combine the mayonnaise, egg, parsley, basil, oregano, dill weed, capers, onion, garlic, lemon juice, horseradish and Worcestershire sauce in a bowl and mix well or process in a food processor or blender for a smoother texture. The sauce can be prepared 1 day in advance and stored in the refrigerator. Stir before serving.

For the cocktail sauce, combine the ketchup, horseradish, Roasted Garlic, lemon juice and Worcestershire sauce in a bowl and mix well. The garlic can be roasted 1 to 2 days in advance. The sauce may be stored in the refrigerator for up to 1 week.

For the shrimp, prepare an ice bath in a large bowl. Bring 3 cups water, the adobo seasoning, salt, pepper and bay leaf to a boil in a saucepan over medium-high heat. Place the shrimp in a steamer basket over the boiling liquid and cover tightly. Steam until the shrimp turn pink. Submerge the shrimp in the ice bath to stop the cooking process; drain. Multiple batches of the shrimp may be steamed over the same liquid. Replenish the water for steaming and for the ice water bath as needed. Serve immediately or chill, covered, for several hours before serving.

Yield: 12 to 20 servings

STONE CRAB CLAWS WITH SPICY MUSTARD SAUCE

As the heat of summer fades into the holidays, celebrate the arrival of stone crab season with a mound of claws served alongside our zesty sauce.

1 cup mayonnaise
1 tablespoon grainy mustard
2 tablespoons heavy cream
1 tablespoon Key lime juice

1/2 teaspoon minced capers
5 pounds stone crab claws, size
    according to preference and budget

Combine the mayonnaise, mustard, cream, Key lime juice and capers in a bowl and mix well. Chill, covered, until serving time. Warm the crab claws by dipping in boiling water in a stockpot for 1 minute. Serve with the sauce. Expect to serve about 1 pound of stone crab claws per person as an appetizer or 1 1/2 pounds per person as an entrée.

Yield: 5 servings

STONE CRABS

Florida stone crab claws are a seasonal treat, available from mid-October to mid-May. Crabbers harvest one claw from each crab, which will regenerate in twelve to eighteen months. If the claws are chilled before they are cooked, the meat will stick to the shell, so they are always sold fully cooked. Claws are sold by size; expect six to seven medium claws per pound, four or five large claws per pound, or two or three jumbo claws per pound. Colossal claws can weigh over seven ounces per claw!

LAYERED SHRIMP DIP

A lighter Gulf Coast take on the traditional layered dip.

8 ounces cream cheese, softened
2 tablespoons sour cream
2 teaspoons Worcestershire sauce
1 teaspoon lemon juice
1 garlic clove, minced
1 cup (4 ounces) shredded Mexican
cheese blend

3 tablespoons chili sauce
1/2 red bell pepper, chopped
10 black olives, chopped (optional)
20 to 30 cooked medium shrimp,
each cut into 4 pieces
3 green onions, chopped

Beat the cream cheese and sour cream in a bowl until smooth. Add the Worcestershire sauce, lemon juice, garlic and 1/2 cup of the cheese and mix well. Spread in a 1-quart serving dish. Layer the chili sauce, remaining 1/2 cup cheese, the bell pepper and olives over the cream cheese mixture. Top with the shrimp. Garnish with the green onions. Serve with corn chips or pita chips.

Yield: 8 to 10 servings

HAMWICH

The original Hamwich recipe was published in The Gasparilla Cookbook *in 1961, and versions have been served in Tampa homes ever since. Easy to prepare in advance and always a crowd pleaser.*

3 tablespoons butter, melted
2 teaspoons mustard
2 teaspoons poppy seeds
1/3 cup chopped onion

Dash of Worcestershire sauce
1 (16-ounce) package frozen dinner rolls
1/3 pound shaved ham
2/3 cup shredded Swiss cheese

Preheat the oven to 350 degrees. Mix the butter, mustard, poppy seeds, onion and Worcestershire sauce in a bowl. Remove the rolls in one piece from the foil pan and cut into halves horizontally. Replace the bottom half in the foil pan and spread evenly with the poppy seed mixture. Layer the ham and cheese over the bottom half of the rolls. Replace the top half of the rolls cut side down over the cheese. Cut into individual servings. Bake for 20 to 25 minutes or until light brown. The rolls may be frozen before baking.

Yield: 16 servings

PECAN-CRUSTED PORK CROSTINI

Strawberry jam provides a sweet contrast for the savory pork in this hearty appetizer.

TOPPING
8 ounces cream cheese, softened
1/4 cup mayonnaise
2 tablespoons fresh thyme, minced
1 to 2 tablespoons fresh chives, minced

1/4 cup packed brown sugar
1/2 teaspoon salt
1/4 teaspoon red pepper flakes
2 (1-pound) pork tenderloins,
    trimmed

PORK
2 eggs
1/2 cup ground pecans
1/2 cup bread crumbs

CROSTINI
1 French baguette
3/4 cup strawberry jam

For the topping, combine the cream cheese, mayonnaise, thyme and chives in a small bowl and mix well. Chill, covered, in the refrigerator.

For the pork, preheat the oven to 375 degrees. Line a rimmed baking sheet with heavy-duty foil and lightly grease. Beat the eggs lightly in a shallow dish. Combine the pecans, bread crumbs, brown sugar, salt and red pepper flakes in a bowl and mix well. Dip the pork in the eggs to coat. Dredge in the pecan mixture to completely cover. Place on the prepared baking sheet. Bake for 30 to 40 minutes or to 160 degrees on a meat thermometer. Let stand for 10 minutes. Cut into slices 1/4 inch thick.

For the crostini, reduce the oven temperature to 350 degrees. Slice the baguette into rounds and place on a baking sheet. Bake until light brown. Spread the cream cheese mixture over each toasted round. Place a slice of pork over the cream cheese mixture. Top each with 1 teaspoon strawberry jam. Serve immediately.

Yield: 18 servings

TENDERLOIN SLIDERS WITH ROASTED GARLIC LIME SAUCE

You are bound to get compliments on this satisfying party appetizer.
Plus, it's great the next day.

ROASTED GARLIC LIME SAUCE
1/2 cup sour cream
2 tablespoons mayonnaise
2 tablespoons Roasted Garlic (page 43)
1 teaspoon Worcestershire sauce
1 teaspoon fresh lime juice
1/2 teaspoon fresh thyme leaves
Kosher salt to taste
Freshly ground pepper to taste

SLIDERS
1/2 cup tequila
1/4 cup vegetable oil
1 tablespoon lime zest
1/4 cup fresh lime juice
1 teaspoon salt
1 teaspoon pepper
4 pounds beef tenderloin
24 small rolls, split and toasted

For the sauce, combine the sour cream, mayonnaise, Roasted Garlic, Worcestershire sauce, lime juice, thyme, salt and pepper in a bowl and mix well. Chill, covered, until serving time. The sauce may be stored in the refrigerator for 2 to 3 days.

For the sliders, whisk the tequila, oil, lime zest, lime juice, salt and pepper in a small bowl. Place the beef in a large sealable plastic bag. Add the tequila mixture and seal the bag. Marinate in the refrigerator for 2 hours. Preheat the oven to 425 degrees. Drain the beef, discarding the marinade. Place the beef on a rack in a roasting pan, tucking the ends under for uniform thickness. Roast for 10 minutes. Reduce the oven temperature to 350 degrees. Roast for 25 minutes longer for rare or 35 minutes longer for medium. Let rest for at least 15 minutes before slicing. Spread the sauce over the bottom half of the rolls. Top each with a slice of beef. Replace with the top halves of the rolls. Serve immediately.

Yield: 24 servings

BACON-WRAPPED STUFFED DATES

Salty bacon and creamy mascarpone cheese, contrasted with the sticky sweetness of dates, make a delicious one-bite appetizer, excellent for cocktail parties.

1/3 cup mascarpone cheese   6 slices bacon
18 pitted Medjool dates

Preheat the oven to 425 degrees. Soak eighteen wooden picks in water in a bowl. Stir the cheese in a bowl until soft. Place in a pastry bag with a small tip or in a small sealable bag with a small corner removed. Pipe the cheese into each date. Cut the bacon into 2¹/₂- to 3-inch strips, depending on the size of the dates. Place a stuffed date in the center of each bacon strip and fold up so the bacon ends overlap slightly. Hold the top and bottom ends of each date to prevent the cheese from escaping and insert a wooden pick at a downward angle through the overlapped bacon and out the back. Slide the date up to the middle of the wooden pick. Place 1 inch apart on a rimmed baking sheet. Bake for 5 minutes. Turn and bake for 5 to 6 minutes longer or until the bacon is crisp; drain. Serve immediately.

Yield: 6 servings

ROASTED GARLIC

Preheat the oven to 450 degrees. Remove the excess papery skin from one head of garlic and cut ¹/₂ inch off the top. Place the garlic in the center of a piece of foil with the shiny side up. Drizzle with ¹/₂ teaspoon olive oil and sprinkle with salt and pepper to taste. Bring up the corners of the foil and twist together to form a pouch. Roast for 20 to 25 minutes or until the garlic is soft and golden caramel in color. Remove from the oven to cool. Squeeze the garlic from the root end; the soft garlic from the cloves should slip out easily. Each head of garlic will yield about 2 tablespoons roasted garlic.

FLORIDA AVOCADO SALSA

This colorful, chunky salsa celebrates the alligator pear, better known as the Florida avocado. When unavailable, substitute Haas avocados.

2 large Florida avocados, pitted and chopped
3 small tomatoes, chopped
1/2 purple onion, chopped

4 ounces crumbled blue cheese or feta cheese
Dash of hot pepper sauce
2 tablespoons red wine vinegar
1/4 cup chopped cilantro (optional)

Combine the avocados, tomatoes and onion in a bowl and toss well. Add the cheese, hot sauce and vinegar and toss gently. Stir in the cilantro. Serve with tortilla chips.

Yield: 8 servings

SPANAKOPITA PHYLLO CUPS

This bite-size appetizer is an appealing take on the classic Greek spanakopita, also known as "Greek spinach pie."

1 (10-ounce) package frozen chopped spinach, thawed and drained
1 cup chopped onion
2 tablespoons olive oil
1 tablespoon chopped fresh dill weed
4 ounces crumbled feta cheese
1 tablespoon all-purpose flour

2 eggs, lightly beaten
1/4 teaspoon grated or ground nutmeg
Dash of salt
1/3 cup slivered almonds
3 (15-count) packages frozen phyllo shells

Preheat the oven to 350 degrees. Squeeze any excess moisture from the spinach. Sauté the onion in the olive oil in a skillet until tender. Add the spinach and dill weed and mix well. Remove from the heat. Stir in the cheese, flour, eggs, nutmeg, salt and almonds. Spoon into the phyllo shells. Bake for 20 minutes or until brown on top. The spinach filling may be prepared a day in advance and stored in the refrigerator.

Yield: 15 servings

MUSHROOM AND GOAT CHEESE TART

*This uncomplicated mushroom filling comes from an old family recipe. Baked into
our rustic tart, it makes a versatile appetizer or a light supper entrée. You can also enjoy the
filling as a spread with crackers or toasted bread rounds.*

MUSHROOM FILLING	TART
8 ounces baby bella mushrooms	1 refrigerator pie pastry
3/4 cup coarsely chopped onion	1/3 cup crumbled goat cheese
2 tablespoons unsalted butter	Leaves from 3 or 4 sprigs of
Salt to taste	fresh thyme
1/2 teaspoon fresh thyme leaves	
1 teaspoon fresh lemon juice	
1 tablespoon mayonnaise	
1/2 teaspoon Worcestershire sauce	

For the spread, rinse the mushrooms and pat dry. Trim the ends from the mushrooms and cut into quarters. Pulse the mushrooms and onion in a food processor until finely chopped. Heat a 10-inch skillet over medium heat; place the butter in the heated skillet. Add the mushroom mixture, salt and thyme when the butter stops sizzling. Sauté over medium-high heat for 5 minutes or until the edges begin to brown. Reduce the heat to low. Sauté for 5 minutes longer or until most of the moisture has evaporated and the mixture forms a smooth paste. Spoon into a small bowl. Let stand until slightly cool. Add the lemon juice, mayonnaise and Worcestershire sauce and mix well. The filling may be made 1 day in advance.

For the tart, preheat the oven to 450 degrees. Remove the pie pastry from the refrigerator and let stand for about 15 minutes. Unroll the pie pastry onto a baking sheet lined with baking parchment. Spread the mushroom filling evenly to within 1 1/2 inches from the edge. Sprinkle with the cheese and thyme. Begin with one edge of the pastry and fold in towards the center, covering part of the mushroom filling. Work around the edge, pleating in about 2-inch sections as you go. When complete, there should be a 4-inch circle of the mushroom filling showing in the middle of the tart and about eight or nine pleats around the edge. Bake on the middle oven rack for 10 minutes. Reduce the oven temperature to 350 degrees. Bake for 20 to 25 minutes longer or until the pastry is golden brown. Remove from the oven and cool on a wire rack for 10 minutes before serving. Serve warm or at room temperature.

Yield: 6 servings

CURRIED EGG SALAD TEA SANDWICHES

Everyone will love this fresh take on an old Southern classic.

4 hard-cooked eggs, peeled and chopped
1/3 cup shredded Swiss cheese
1/4 cup chopped onion
2 tablespoons chopped sweet pickles or pickle relish
2 teaspoons fresh lemon juice
3 tablespoons mayonnaise

1/2 teaspoon curry powder
1/4 teaspoon salt
Pinch of white pepper
2 tablespoons butter, softened
12 slices thin white bread or rye bread
1 cup watercress, tough stems removed

Combine the eggs, cheese, onion, pickles, lemon juice, mayonnaise, curry powder, salt and white pepper in a bowl and mix well. Spread the butter on one side of each bread slice. Spread the egg salad on half the bread slices and top each with several sprigs of the watercress. Top with the remaining bread slices buttered side down. Cut each sandwich into triangles and place on a serving tray. Cover with a damp paper towel and then plastic wrap. Chill for 1 hour before serving.

Yield: 24 servings

MINI TOMATO ROUNDS

This simple appetizer will earn rave reviews at your next gathering.

1/4 cup mayonnaise
3 ounces cream cheese, softened
1 tablespoon chopped fresh basil
1/4 teaspoon sea salt

1/4 teaspoon freshly ground pepper
1 French baguette
4 plum tomatoes, sliced

Preheat the oven to 350 degrees. Combine the mayonnaise, cream cheese, basil, 1/8 teaspoon of the salt and 1/8 teaspoon of the pepper in a bowl and mix well. Chill, covered, until serving time. Slice the baguette into sixteen rounds. Place on a baking sheet. Bake until toasted. Spread each round with the cream cheese spread. Top each with a tomato slice. Sprinkle with the remaining salt and pepper.

Yield: 16 servings

DILL DIP

Most kitchens already have these ingredients on hand. Serve along with your favorite crudités for an easy snack; it makes a nice spread for sandwiches as well.

$1/2$ cup sour cream
$2/3$ cup mayonnaise
1 to 2 tablespoons grated onion
1 tablespoon dried parsley
1 teaspoon seasoned salt

1 teaspoon dried dill weed, or
2 to 3 tablespoons fresh dill weed
$1/2$ teaspoon Worcestershire sauce
Dash of Tabasco sauce

Combine the sour cream, mayonnaise, onion, parsley, seasoned salt, dill weed, Worcestershire sauce and Tabasco sauce in a bowl and mix well. Chill, covered, for 8 to 10 hours before serving. You may use lower-fat sour cream and mayonnaise in this recipe.

Yield: 8 to 10 servings

FISH AND BUBBLES PARTY MIX

This fun snack mix will be devoured by children and adults alike. The saltiness of the mix and the praline flavor of the coating yield a festive flavor that everyone will enjoy.

5 cups crispy corn and rice cereal,
such as Chex
3 cups Cheerios
4 cups fish-shaped cheese crackers
2 cups fish-shaped pretzel nuggets

1 cup peanuts
$1 1/2$ cups pecan halves or pieces
1 cup (2 sticks) butter
1 cup packed brown sugar
2 cups "M & M's" Chocolate Candies

Preheat the oven to 250 degrees. Combine the cereals, crackers, pretzel nuggets, peanuts and pecan halves in a large bowl and mix well. Bring the butter and brown sugar to a boil in a saucepan. Boil until frothy, stirring constantly. Pour over the cereal mixture and toss to coat. Spread evenly in a large roasting pan. Bake for 10 minutes and stir. Continue baking for 45 minutes, stirring once or twice. Remove from the oven and cool to room temperature. Add the chocolate candies and toss well. Store in an airtight container.

Yield: 36 servings

SIDES & SUCH

PARADISE SALAD

*This vibrant salad is full of fresh local produce. The creamy tropical
dressing is reminiscent of a piña colada.*

2 (5-ounce) packages spring salad mix
4 cups chopped fresh pineapple
2 cups sliced strawberries
1 1/2 cups grapes, cut into halves
2 cups blueberries
2 cups chopped Granny Smith apples
1 star fruit, thinly sliced crosswise

1/2 cup honey-roasted slivered almonds
3/4 cup mayonnaise
1/4 cup sour cream
1 (8.5-ounce) can cream of coconut
3 tablespoons lime juice
2 tablespoons apricot preserves

Combine the salad mix, pineapple, strawberries, grapes, blueberries, apples, star fruit and almonds
in a large salad bowl and toss to mix. Whisk the mayonnaise, sour cream, cream of coconut, lime juice
and apricot preserves in a bowl until blended. Serve the salad with the dressing on the side. The dressing
may be made in advance and stored in the refrigerator until serving time. Sprinkle the chopped apples
with lemon juice to prevent browning. The honey-roasted slivered almonds may be found in the produce
section of your favorite grocery.

Yield: 8 to 10 servings

PEELING A PINEAPPLE

*Cut off the leaves and about a half inch of the top and bottom,
creating two flat ends. Stand the pineapple on one flat edge. Using a
sawing motion, cut from top to bottom following the curve of the
fruit to remove the rough husk of the pineapple. To remove the
inedible core, cut the fruit from top to bottom into quarters and lay
each piece on its side. Cut down at an angle to remove the core.*

FARMHOUSE SALAD
WITH BASIL LIME VINAIGRETTE

*Grape tomatoes and sweet corn are farm stand favorites, paired here
with a refreshing citrus and herb dressing.*

BASIL LIME VINAIGRETTE
Juice of 2 limes
3 tablespoons honey
2 tablespoons chopped basil
3/4 cup olive oil
Salt and pepper to taste

SALAD
1 head romaine, rinsed and torn
2 cups fresh spinach leaves
1/2 cup shaved red onion
1/2 cup fresh or thawed frozen whole
   kernel corn
1 cup grape tomatoes, cut into halves

For the vinaigrette, mix the lime juice, honey and basil in a medium bowl. Whisk in the olive oil gradually. Season with salt and pepper.

For the salad, combine the romaine, spinach, onion, corn and tomatoes in a salad bowl. Add the vinaigrette to taste and toss to coat. You may add grilled chicken, pork, steak or shrimp to serve as an entrée.

Yield: 8 servings

SQUEEZING A LEMON OR LIME

Microwave a lemon or lime for five or ten seconds before

cutting and squeezing to increase the amount of juice that comes

from the lemon or lime.

CHICK-PEA AND SPINACH SALAD

In our interpretation of a modern Mediterranean salad, ingredients like garbanzo beans, spinach, feta cheese, and pine nuts combine in a culinary tribute to Tampa's historic cultural influences.

GREEK DRESSING
6 tablespoons extra-virgin olive oil
2 tablespoons red wine vinegar
1 teaspoon crushed dried oregano
1/4 teaspoon onion powder
1/4 teaspoon garlic powder
1/2 teaspoon kosher salt
Freshly ground pepper to taste

SALAD
1/2 cup pine nuts
5 ounces baby spinach
1 cup chick-peas, drained and rinsed
1 Roasted Red Bell Pepper,
    cut into strips (below)
1/2 cup crumbled feta cheese

For the dressing, whisk the olive oil, vinegar, oregano, onion powder, garlic power, salt and pepper in a bowl until blended or place in a jar with a tight-fitting lid and shake to mix well.

For the salad, toast the pine nuts in a small skillet over medium-low heat for 3 to 4 minutes, stirring and shaking the skillet to brown evenly. Spread in a single layer on a plate to cool. Combine the spinach, chick-peas, roasted bell pepper, cheese and pine nuts in a salad bowl. Add the dressing and toss to coat. You may use one 12-ounce jar roasted red bell peppers, drained, instead of roasting your own.

Yield: 6 servings

ROASTED RED BELL PEPPERS

To roast red bell peppers, place the whole bell pepper on

the grating directly above a gas burner on medium-high heat. Roast until

the bell pepper is charred and blackened, turning occasionally.

Place the bell pepper in a plastic shopping bag and tie the handles in

a knot. Steam in the bag for 10 to 15 minutes or until the skin

loosens. Remove the skin and seed.

COLUMBIA RESTAURANT'S "1905" SALAD

*Founded in 1905 by Casimiro Hernandez Sr., the Columbia Restaurant is
a renowned Spanish restaurant in Tampa's historic Ybor City. Today the oldest restaurant
in Florida is run by fourth- and fifth-generation restaurateurs, brothers Richard and
Casey Gonzmart and their children. The famous "1905" Salad is an authentic
taste from a true Tampa institution.*

"1905" SALAD DRESSING
4 garlic cloves, minced
1 teaspoon oregano
1 teaspoon Worcestershire sauce
1/2 cup extra-virgin Spanish olive oil
2 tablespoons white wine vinegar
2 teaspoons lemon juice
Salt and pepper to taste

SALAD
1/2 head iceberg lettuce
2 tomatoes, cut into eighths
1/2 cup julienned Swiss cheese
1/2 cup julienned ham, turkey or shrimp
1/4 cup pitted green Spanish olives
2 teaspoons grated Romano cheese

For the dressing, whisk the garlic, oregano and Worcestershire sauce in a bowl. Add the olive oil gradually, whisking constantly until emulsified. Whisk in the vinegar, lemon juice, salt and pepper.

For the salad, combine the lettuce, tomatoes, Swiss cheese, ham and olives in a bowl. Add the dressing and toss to coat. Add the Romano cheese and toss again.

Yield: 4 servings

MANGO-CHILI BAY SCALLOP SALAD

*Tender and sweet bay scallops are wonderful paired with mango and an
Asian-inspired dressing. Serve this main course salad with crusty bread or a small bowl of
jasmine rice for a light and healthy summer supper.*

MANGO SALAD DRESSING
1/4 cup mango nectar
1 tablespoon brown sugar
1 tablespoon mirin
1 tablespoon sesame oil
1 tablespoon canola oil
1 tablespoon minced shallot
1 teaspoon minced garlic
1/2 teaspoon hot pepper sauce
1/4 teaspoon kosher salt
1/4 teaspoon dry mustard

SALAD
1 pound bay scallops
Salt and pepper to taste
2 teaspoons all-purpose flour
1 tablespoon honey
1 tablespoon mango nectar
2 teaspoons fresh lemon juice
1/4 teaspoon hot pepper sauce
1 tablespoon each butter and olive oil
1/4 teaspoon minced garlic
1 tablespoon minced shallot
1 (5-ounce) package mixed salad greens
1 1/2 to 2 cups ripe mangoes, chopped
3/4 cup chopped red bell pepper

For the dressing, whisk the nectar, brown sugar, mirin, sesame oil, canola oil, shallot, garlic, hot sauce, salt and dry mustard in a bowl until blended or place in a jar with a tight-fitting lid and shake to mix well. The dressing may be made in advance. Mirin is a sweet rice wine found in Asian markets.

For the salad, drain the scallops and pat dry with paper towels to remove excess moisture. Season with salt and pepper. Combine with the flour in a bowl and toss to coat. Mix the honey, nectar, lemon juice and hot sauce in a small bowl. Melt the butter with the olive oil in a 10- or 12-inch skillet over medium-high heat. Add the scallops in a single layer when the butter stops sizzling. Cook for 1 minute or until light brown. Stir the scallops. Cook for 1 to 2 minutes longer or until cooked through. Remove the scallops with a slotted spoon to a plate or bowl. Reduce the heat to medium. Add the garlic and shallot to the drippings in the skillet and sauté for 1 minute. Reduce the heat to low. Add the honey mixture, stirring to scrape up any brown bits. Cook for 1 to 2 minutes or until the liquid is syrupy. Return the scallops to the skillet and stir to coat. Remove the skillet from the heat. Place the salad greens in a salad bowl. Add the dressing and toss to coat. Divide among four salad bowls. Top with the mangoes and bell pepper. Spoon the scallops over the top.

Yield: 4 servings

MELON, CUCUMBER AND TOMATO SALAD

Perfect for summer barbecues, this salad is crisp, cool, and refreshing.

DRESSING	SALAD
1/2 cup extra-virgin olive oil	3 cups (1/4-inch chunks) peeled
1/4 cup white balsamic vinegar	cucumbers
2 tablespoons minced shallot	Salt to taste
1/2 teaspoon Dijon mustard	3 cups (1/4-inch chunks) cantaloupe
1/2 teaspoon kosher salt, or to taste	3 cups grape tomato halves
1/4 teaspoon garlic powder	1/2 cup chopped or thinly sliced
Freshly ground pepper to taste	mint leaves

For the dressing, combine the olive oil, vinegar, shallot, Dijon mustard, salt, garlic powder and pepper in a jar with a tight-fitting lid. Secure the lid and shake well.

For the salad, place the cucumbers in a colander or large strainer. Sprinkle with salt and toss well. Let stand in the colander over a bowl or soup dish for 30 minutes to drain the excess moisture. Rinse briefly and pat dry with paper towels. Combine the cucumbers, cantaloupe, tomatoes and mint in a serving bowl. Chill until serving time. Add the dressing just before serving and toss to coat.

Yield: 6 servings

SNORKELING FOR SCALLOPS

Snorkeling for Florida bay scallops is a popular

summer activity. Scallops live in and around grass flats in shallow

water, no more than ten feet deep. Unlike clams and

oysters, scallops do not live long out of water and should be placed

on ice immediately and shucked as soon as possible.

BLACK BEAN MANGO SALAD

A burst of tropical flavors! Wonderful as an accompaniment to grilled fish or seafood, it doubles as a dip with tortilla chips.

1/4 cup orange juice	1 cup chopped seeded plum tomatoes
2 tablespoons Key lime juice or lime juice	1/2 cup chopped red onion
1/2 teaspoon grated minced ginger	1/2 cup chopped green or red bell pepper
1 (15-ounce) can black beans, drained and rinsed	1/4 cup chopped cilantro
1 1/2 cups chopped mangoes	1 tablespoon minced seeded jalapeño chile
	1 teaspoon kosher salt

Blend the orange juice and Key lime juice in a microwave-safe bowl. Microwave for 30 seconds. Stir in the ginger and black beans. Microwave for 30 seconds. Cool to room temperature.

Combine the mangoes, tomatoes, onion, bell pepper, cilantro, jalapeño chile and salt in a large bowl and stir gently. Stir in the black bean mixture gently. Chill until serving time. Serve chilled or at room temperature.

Yield: 6 servings

MANGO CAPRESE

Try this exotic variation on the classic Caprese salad.

Peel and slice 2 ripe mangoes. Cut an 8-ounce ball of fresh

mozzarella cheese into slices. Layer the mango and cheese

slices on a salad plate. Drizzle with good-quality balsamic vinegar

and sprinkle with chopped cilantro, if desired.

ASPARAGUS AND CITRUS SALAD

*This colorful salad showcases Florida oranges paired with asparagus for
a simple, yet sophisticated salad.*

CITRUS VINAIGRETTE
1/4 cup red wine vinegar
1/4 cup orange juice or lemon juice
2 teaspoons Dijon mustard
1/2 teaspoon grated orange zest
Salt and pepper to taste
1/2 cup peanut oil or olive oil

SALAD
2 pounds small asparagus spears,
   trimmed
Salt to taste
2 large oranges
1/2 cup thinly sliced red onion
1/2 cup crumbled blue cheese

For the vinaigrette, combine the vinegar, orange juice, Dijon mustard, orange zest, salt and pepper in a bowl and mix well. Whisk in the peanut oil.

For the salad, cook the asparagus in boiling salted water in a saucepan for 3 to 5 minutes or until tender-crisp. Drain and immediately plunge into ice water to stop the cooking process. Let stand until cool. Drain the asparagus and cut into small pieces. To section the oranges, cut a thin slice from the stem end and opposite end to create a flat surface. Cut the side of each orange in a curved motion to remove the peel. Hold the orange in the palm of your hand and cut on either side of the dividing membranes. Lift out the section and remove any seeds. Combine the asparagus, oranges, onion and cheese in a large bowl. Add the vinaigrette and toss to coat.

Yield: 4 to 6 servings

MEDITERRANEAN ORZO SALAD

With Greek and Italian influences, this dish really steals the show.
Your family won't get enough.

1/4 cup good-quality olive oil
1/4 cup fresh lemon juice
Zest of 1 lemon
1 tablespoon minced garlic
1 teaspoon dried oregano
1 teaspoon salt
1/4 teaspoon pepper
1/2 cup sugar
2 cups orzo
1/2 cup pine nuts

1/2 cup golden raisins
6 tablespoons finely chopped pitted
    black olives (optional)
6 tablespoons finely chopped shallots or
    red onion
1/2 cup thinly sliced fresh basil
4 ounces feta cheese, drained
    and crumbled
Salt and pepper to taste

Whisk the olive oil, lemon juice, lemon zest, garlic, oregano, 1 teaspoon salt, 1/4 teaspoon pepper and the sugar in a small bowl. Cook the pasta using the package directions; drain.

Place the pine nuts in a dry small skillet. Cook over medium-low heat for 5 minutes or until evenly toasted, shaking the skillet constantly.

Combine the pasta and dressing in a medium bowl and toss to coat. Cool to room temperature, stirring occasionally. Add the pine nuts, raisins, olives, shallots and basil and mix well. Add the cheese and toss lightly. Season with salt and pepper.

Yield: 12 servings

SHRIMP PASTA SALAD

Looking for something to do with leftover shrimp? This pasta salad will wake up precooked or grilled shrimp.

2 cups spiral tri-colored pasta
1 cup chopped cooked shrimp
1/3 cup chopped green bell pepper
1/4 cup sliced carrots
1/2 cup sliced zucchini
1/3 cup mayonnaise

1/4 cup ketchup
1/4 cup chopped flat-leaf parsley
1 tablespoon capers
1 tablespoon lemon juice
Salt and pepper to taste
Lemon wedges to taste

Cook the pasta using the package directions; drain. Combine the pasta, shrimp, bell pepper, carrots and zucchini in a large bowl. Mix the mayonnaise, ketchup, parsley, capers and lemon juice in a bowl. Add to the pasta mixture and toss to coat. Add salt and pepper and toss lightly. Chill for 30 minutes or longer before serving. Squeeze juice from lemon wedges over the salad just before serving.

Yield: 4 servings

SHRIMP VARIETIES

Wild-caught Florida shrimp are harvested by trawlers, often fishing at night with a light to attract the shrimp. Pink Gulf shrimp are the most common, but white, brown, and royal red shrimp are also caught in shallow waters off both coasts of the state. Rock shrimp are a deep-water species found along the Atlantic Coast. They have thick shells and rich meat like little lobsters.

FLORIDA LOBSTER SALAD

A member was kind enough to pass along this old family recipe featuring the prized Florida lobster. It's delicious on fresh Cuban bread or served over a bed of greens.

6 Florida lobster tails, peeled and
cut into halves lengthwise
1/2 cup mayonnaise
1 tablespoon French salad dressing
1 tablespoon lime juice
6 green onions, thinly sliced

3 ribs celery, thinly sliced
1/2 cup chopped green olives
3 hard-cooked eggs, chopped
2 teaspoons cilantro, chopped
Kosher salt and cracked pepper to taste

Cook the lobster in boiling water in a large saucepan for 7 to 12 minutes or until opaque. Drain and chill. Cut into 1/2-inch pieces. Mix the mayonnaise, salad dressing and lime juice in a bowl. Add the lobster, green onions, celery, olives, eggs, cilantro, salt and pepper and mix well. Chill for 30 minutes before serving.

Yield: 8 servings

SEAFOOD CORN BREAD

*Cut into bite-size squares to serve as an easy appetizer or into larger squares
to serve as a hearty side with your favorite entrée.*

3 eggs
1 (8-ounce) package corn bread mix
1 cup chopped onion
1 cup chopped green onions

1 cup (4 ounces) shredded Colby cheese
1 cup chopped tomatoes
1/2 cup (1 stick) butter, melted
8 ounces lump crab meat, drained well

Preheat the oven to 350 degrees. Combine the eggs, corn bread mix, onion, green onions, cheese, tomatoes and butter in a bowl and mix well. Stir in the crab meat. Spoon into a greased 9×13-inch glass baking dish. Bake for 50 to 55 minutes or until firm.

Yield: 16 servings

WRIGHT'S DILL POTATO SALAD

Wright's Gourmet House is a South Tampa institution known for its hearty sandwiches, mouth-watering cakes, and fabulous salads.

2 pounds red Bliss potatoes	1 tablespoon fresh dill weed
Salt to taste	1/4 cup sour cream
2/3 cup mayonnaise	Finely ground white pepper to taste

Cut the potatoes into 3/4-inch pieces and place in a saucepan. Add salted water to cover the potatoes by 1 inch. Cook until the potatoes are tender. Drain the potatoes and place on a rimmed baking sheet. Chill in the refrigerator. Combine half the mayonnaise and the dill weed in a small bowl and mix well. Add the sour cream and remaining mayonnaise and mix well. Combine with the potatoes, salt and white pepper in a large bowl and mix gently.

Yield: 4 to 6 servings

HONEY LIME SWEET POTATO SALAD

Cilantro and lime balance the hearty flavor of roasted sweet potatoes, making this a delightful side dish all year long.

3 pounds sweet potatoes, peeled	2 tablespoons fresh lime juice
3 tablespoons olive oil	1 tablespoon orange juice
1/2 teaspoon salt	1/4 teaspoon coarse salt
2 tablespoons Florida orange	3/4 cup pecan halves, toasted
blossom honey	1/4 cup cilantro, chopped

Preheat the oven to 400 degrees. Cut each sweet potato into halves lengthwise. Cut each half into quarters. Cut crosswise into 2-inch pieces. Toss with 2 tablespoons of the olive oil and 1/2 teaspoon salt. Spread in a single layer on a large baking sheet lined with baking parchment. Roast for 30 to 40 minutes or until tender. Remove from the oven to cool. Mix the honey, lime juice, orange juice, remaining 1 tablespoon olive oil and 1/4 teaspoon coarse salt in a small bowl. Combine the sweet potatoes, honey mixture, pecans and cilantro in a bowl and toss gently. Serve at room temperature.

Yield: 6 servings

GRILLED CORN WITH HERBED COMPOUND BUTTER

When a kitchen is unavailable or you just want to turn off your stove,
try this flavorful preparation for fresh corn.

8 ears fresh corn	3 tablespoons chopped cilantro
1/2 cup (1 stick) unsalted	1 teaspoon lime zest
butter, softened	1/2 teaspoon salt

Preheat the grill. Pull back the corn husks, leaving them attached to the base. Remove the silks. Reposition the husks. Soak in ice water in a bowl for 10 minutes; drain. Place the corn on a grill rack. Grill, covered, over medium heat for 15 minutes. Combine the butter, cilantro, lime zest and salt in a bowl and mix well. Pull back the corn husks and spread each ear with 1 tablespoon of the herbed butter. Serve immediately or reposition the husks and keep warm. The herbed butter may be shaped into a log and stored in the refrigerator or freezer until serving time. Parsley, salt and pepper will make a traditional compound butter. Mix chives, chili powder and lime zest for a spicy option.

Yield: 8 servings

GRILLED BANANAS

Heat 1/2 cup molasses and 1/4 cup honey in a saucepan. Add
2 tablespoons dark rum. Cook over medium-high heat for 5 minutes.
Peel and cut four firm or just ripened bananas lengthwise into slices.
Sprinkle with a mixture of 1 teaspoon cinnamon, 1/2 teaspoon ground
cloves, and 1/2 teaspoon nutmeg. Brush with half the honey mixture.
Place the bananas on a grill rack. Grill until tender. Brush with the
remaining honey mixture before serving. Use as an interesting
side dish or serve warm over ice cream for a big finish.

SWEET-AND-SOUR GREEN BEANS

Give farm-fresh green beans a little zip with a quick-and-easy
sauce and a sprinkle of almonds.

1 pound green beans, trimmed
2 tablespoons lemon juice
1 tablespoon cider vinegar
1 tablespoon sugar
1/2 teaspoon kosher salt

1 tablespoon unsalted butter
1 tablespoon chopped green onions
Kosher salt and pepper to taste
1/4 cup slivered almonds

Steam the green beans in a steamer for 4 minutes. Place in a bowl. Cover and set aside. Mix the lemon juice, vinegar, sugar and 1/2 teaspoon salt in a bowl. Melt the butter in a skillet over medium heat. Add the green onions. Sauté for 2 minutes or until tender but not brown. Stir in the lemon juice mixture. Bring to a boil. Boil for 1 to 2 minutes or until slightly thickened. Add the green beans and toss to coat. Sprinkle with salt and pepper to taste. Spoon into a serving bowl. Sprinkle with the almonds.

Yield: 4 servings

VEGETABLE GRILL PACKS

Combine 3 cups chopped vegetables with 2 tablespoons fresh thyme
in a bowl. Drizzle with olive oil and toss to combine. Divide the
mixture among four to six 20-inch pieces of foil. Fold the foil to
enclose the vegetables, crimping and sealing the foil down the center
and ends. Grill for 5 to 10 minutes or until the vegetables are tender.
Serve with lemon wedges. This works great with zucchini, yellow
squash, red bell peppers, mushrooms, or other assorted vegetables.

ZUCCHINI AND TOMATO GRATIN

This oven-baked side is a "go-to" recipe when you run out of room on the grill.
Great for weeknight dinners or weekend gatherings.

3 beefsteak tomatoes or other tomatoes
1/2 teaspoon kosher salt
2 large zucchini, or 3 medium zucchini
1/4 cup fresh whole basil leaves
1 cup fresh bread crumbs
1/4 cup (1 ounce) grated
   Parmesan cheese
1/2 teaspoon kosher salt

Freshly ground pepper to taste
1 egg
1/2 cup half-and-half
1/4 cup milk
1/4 teaspoon kosher salt
2 tablespoons unsalted butter, cut into
   small pieces

Preheat the oven to 375 degrees. Cut the tomatoes crosswise into 1/4-inch slices. Place in a colander or sieve and set over a bowl. Sprinkle with 1/2 teaspoon salt. Let stand to drain. Trim the ends of the zucchini and cut into halves lengthwise. Cut each half crosswise into 1/8-inch slices. Spread half the zucchini in a greased 8×10-inch or 11/2- to 2-quart baking dish. Stack the basil leaves and roll up. Cut crosswise into 1/8-inch ribbons.

Mix the basil, bread crumbs, cheese, 1/2 teaspoon salt and pepper in a small bowl. Spread half the bread crumb mixture over the zucchini. Continue layering with the remaining zucchini, the tomato slices and the remaining bread crumb mixture. Whisk the egg, half-and-half, milk and 1/4 teaspoon salt in a bowl until smooth. Pour over the layers. Top with the butter. Bake for 40 to 45 minutes or until the top is golden brown.

Yield: 6 to 8 servings

SUMMER VEGETABLES OVER COUSCOUS

For a more robust flavor, let the vegetables marinate for an hour or two before baking.
Colorful enough for a buffet and great served warm or at room temperature.

1/2 cup chopped fresh basil
1/2 cup balsamic vinegar
2 tablespoons extra-virgin olive oil
Salt to taste
3 garlic cloves, finely chopped or crushed
2 zucchini, cut into halves and cut into 1-inch slices
8 ounces whole baby bella mushrooms
1 red onion, cut into 8 wedges
2 bell peppers, cut into 1-inch pieces
3 cups cooked couscous (cooked in chicken stock instead of water)
5 ounces goat cheese or feta cheese, crumbled
Pepper to taste
Fresh basil leaves

Preheat the oven to 425 degrees. Whisk 1/2 cup basil, the vinegar, olive oil, salt and garlic in a small bowl until combined. Place the zucchini, mushrooms, onion and bell peppers in a large sealable plastic bag. Pour the vinegar mixture over the vegetables and seal the bag. Toss to coat the vegetables. Place the undrained vegetables in a shallow roasting pan coated with nonstick cooking spray. Bake for 30 to 35 minutes or until the vegetables are brown and tender, stirring occasionally. Spoon the hot couscous onto a serving platter. Top with the roasted vegetables. Sprinkle with the cheese and pepper. Garnish with fresh basil leaves.

Yield: 4 to 6 servings

Sweet Onion Soufflé

Featuring locally grown sweet onions, this soufflé makes a wonderfully distinctive side dish. It pairs beautifully with grilled meat.

1¹/4 pounds Florida sweet onions
2 tablespoons unsalted butter
4 to 5 cups cubed trimmed white bread
³/4 cup (3 ounces) shredded sharp
　　Cheddar cheese
3 eggs

1 cup light or low-fat buttermilk,
　　well shaken
2 teaspoons kosher salt
¹/4 cup (1 ounce) shredded sharp
　　Cheddar cheese
1 tablespoon brown sugar

Preheat the oven to 350 degrees. Cut the onions into halves lengthwise, leaving the root end attached. Trim the opposite end and peel. Place the onions flat side down and cut into thirds lengthwise, leaving the onion attached at the root end. Cut crosswise into thin slices. You should have about 4 cups of onion slices.

Melt the butter in a 10- or 12-inch skillet over medium heat. Add the onions. Cook for 15 minutes or until tender and completely translucent, reducing the heat if needed to prevent the onions from browning. Remove from the heat and cool slightly. Combine the onions, bread cubes and ³/4 cup cheese in a large bowl and toss to mix. Spoon into a greased 1¹/2-quart soufflé dish or baking dish. Whisk the eggs in a large bowl. Add the buttermilk and salt and whisk until smooth. Pour over the onion mixture. Top with ¹/4 cup cheese. Sprinkle evenly with the brown sugar. Bake for 30 minutes or until set.

To prepare in advance, assemble the soufflé early in the day. Chill, covered with plastic wrap, until serving time. Uncover and let stand at room temperature for 30 minutes before baking. When cutting the bread cubes, only cut one or two slices of bread at a time to keep bread cubes light and fluffy.

Yield: 6 to 8 servings

SUMMER SQUASH BISQUE

Don't tell your guests how easy this beautiful golden soup is to prepare. It looks extra elegant when brought to the table with a dollop of sour cream and a sprig of fresh chives.

1 large onion, chopped
1/2 cup (1 stick) butter
2 potatoes, peeled and chopped
3 carrots, chopped
4 cups sliced yellow squash
4 cups chicken broth
1/2 teaspoon nutmeg
1/4 teaspoon salt
1/4 teaspoon red pepper
1 cup milk
1 cup sour cream
Fresh chives

Sauté the onion in the butter in a large saucepan until tender. Add the potatoes, carrots, squash, broth, nutmeg, salt and red pepper. Cover and reduce the heat. Simmer for 1 hour, stirring occasionally. Process in a food processor or with an immersion blender until smooth. Return to the saucepan. Bring to a boil. Stir in the milk. Cook until heated through. Ladle into soup bowls. Garnish each serving with a dollop of the sour cream and fresh chives.

Yield: 12 servings

FRIJOLES NEGROS

Passed down from a member's Cuban abuela (grandmother), this recipe represents very traditional Cuban fare. The longer the beans cook, the more tender they become.

1 pound dried black beans
2 tablespoons olive oil
1 bay leaf
1/2 cup coarsely chopped onion
1/2 cup coarsely chopped green bell pepper
1 garlic clove, unpeeled and crushed
1/2 cup olive oil
1/2 cup finely chopped onion

1/2 cup finely chopped green bell pepper
2 teaspoons minced garlic
1 teaspoon crushed dried oregano
1/4 teaspoon ground cumin
2 tablespoons red wine vinegar
1 tablespoon salt
1/2 teaspoon hot pepper sauce
2 tablespoons dry sherry
(preferably oloroso or amontillado)

Sort and rinse the beans. Place in a 3- to 4-quart saucepan and add enough water to cover the beans by 2 inches. Soak for 8 to 10 hours. Add 2 tablespoons olive oil, the bay leaf, 1/2 cup coarsely chopped onion, 1/2 cup coarsely chopped bell pepper and the crushed unpeeled garlic. Bring to a boil, skimming off the foam as it rises to the surface. Reduce the heat to medium. Cook, covered, for 1 hour or until the beans are tender, stirring occasionally with a wooden spoon. Discard the bay leaf, onion, bell pepper and garlic.

Heat 1/2 cup olive oil in a skillet. Add 1/2 cup finely chopped onion and 1/2 cup finely chopped bell pepper. Sauté until the onion is translucent. Add the minced garlic, oregano, cumin, vinegar and salt and mix well. Cook for 2 minutes. Stir into the beans. Stir in the hot sauce. Cook, covered, for 30 minutes. Adjust the seasonings to taste. Stir in the sherry. Serve with hot cooked rice and chopped onions, if desired.

Yield: 8 to 16 servings

CALDO GALLEGO

This soup resembles the Spanish classic featured in The Gasparilla Cookbook.
*Adapted from the handwritten notes of a member's mother, this version is quicker to prepare
than the original, while preserving the soup's full flavor.*

1 meaty ham bone or ham hock	1/4 cup olive oil
1 bay leaf	3 red potatoes, chopped
24 cups (6 quarts) water	1 (16-ounce) package frozen
3 links chorizo, sliced	collard greens
3 onions, chopped	3 (15-ounce) cans Great Northern beans
1 bell pepper, chopped	Salt and pepper to taste

Place the ham bone, bay leaf and water in a large stockpot. Add water if needed to cover the ham bone. Bring to a boil. Reduce the heat and simmer for 30 minutes. Sauté the chorizo, onions and bell pepper in the olive oil in a skillet until the vegetables are soft. Remove the ham bone from the water. Chop the ham, discarding the bone. Return the ham to the stockpot. Add the potatoes and collard greens. Bring to a boil. Boil for 10 minutes. Reduce the heat to low. Add the chorizo mixture and beans. Cook, covered, over low heat for 1 to 2 hours, stirring occasionally. Season with salt and pepper. Discard the bay leaf. Ladle into soup bowls.

Yield: 10 to 12 servings

HONEY-BAKED PLANTAINS

*Plantains look like large bananas, but are less sweet and
are starchy like sweet potatoes. A popular Cuban-style dish usually
sautéed in butter or vegetable oil, try baking them in the oven
for a less messy approach. Peel 2 large ripe plantains, cut into
quarters and place in a baking dish. Drizzle with 2 to 3 tablespoons
vegetable oil and 1 tablespoon honey. Sprinkle with salt.
Bake for 30 minutes or until tender.*

FRESH CORN AND SHRIMP BISQUE

*We love this bisque not only for its simplicity but also for the complex body
of flavors and textures found in every spoonful.*

3 tablespoons butter
1/2 cup chopped onion
3 tablespoons all-purpose flour
1 teaspoon salt
1 teaspoon black pepper
3/4 teaspoon cayenne pepper
1 tablespoon Worcestershire sauce
1/2 teaspoon Tabasco sauce

4 cups (1 quart) fat-free half-and-half
1 cup (4 ounces) shredded Mexican or
  Cheddar cheese
1 pound shrimp, peeled and deveined
Corn kernels from 3 boiled ears of corn,
  or 3 cups frozen or canned whole
  kernel corn

Melt the butter in a large saucepan. Add the onion and sauté until translucent. Add the flour gradually, stirring constantly. Stir in the salt, black pepper, cayenne pepper, Worcestershire sauce and Tabasco sauce. Add the half-and-half, stirring gently. Bring to a gentle boil. Reduce the heat. Add the cheese, shrimp and corn. Simmer for 30 minutes. Ladle into soup bowls.

Yield: 8 servings

CROUTONS

Preheat the oven to 350 degrees. Place 5 cups dry Cuban or

French bread cubes in a large bowl. Drizzle with 3 tablespoons olive oil.

Sprinkle with 1/2 teaspoon salt. Toss the bread cubes to coat evenly.

Spread in a single layer on a baking sheet. Bake for 10 minutes and stir.

Bake for 5 to 10 minutes longer or until golden brown and crunchy.

The exact baking time will depend on the dryness of the bread.

Croutons keep well in the refrigerator for about 1 week.

GAZPACHO WITH SHRIMP

*Adding shrimp to a bounty of farm fresh vegetables, this delicious
gazpacho is a cool first course for a waterside dinner.*

3 pounds red ripe tomatoes, peeled,
seeded and coarsely chopped
1 green bell pepper, coarsely chopped
1 small cucumber, peeled, seeded and
coarsely chopped
1 red onion, coarsely chopped
3 green onions, sliced
2 garlic cloves, coarsely chopped
2 tablespoons chopped fresh basil
1 tablespoon chopped fresh cilantro
3 tablespoons extra-virgin olive oil

1 teaspoon rice wine vinegar
1/4 teaspoon cayenne pepper
Pinch of dried oregano
Pinch of kosher salt
Ground white pepper to taste
Adobo seasoning to taste
1 bay leaf (optional)
Salt and black pepper to taste
1 pound shrimp, deveined
4 cups Croutons (page 70)
Chopped fresh basil

Combine the tomatoes, bell pepper, cucumber, red onion, green onions, garlic, 2 tablespoons basil, the cilantro, olive oil, vinegar, cayenne pepper and oregano in a large bowl and mix well. Process in batches in a food processor or blender until combined but still chunky. Place in a large bowl. Sprinkle with salt and white pepper. Chill, covered, for 1 hour or longer.

Place 1 inch of water in a saucepan with a steamer insert. Add adobo seasoning, bay leaf, salt and black pepper to taste. Cover and bring to a boil. Place the shrimp in the steamer insert. Steam, covered, for 3 minutes or until the shrimp turn pink. Spread the shrimp on a plate. Let stand until cool enough to handle. Peel the shrimp. Chop the shrimp coarsely. Chill, covered, until serving time.

To serve, stir the shrimp into the gazpacho. If the gazpacho is too thick, add a small amount of chicken broth or vegetable broth. Ladle into chilled soup plates. Sprinkle with the croutons and garnish with chopped fresh basil. Serve with additional croutons on the side.

Yield: 6 to 8 servings

GRIDDLE CAKES WITH EASY STRAWBERRY SAUCE

The addition of cottage cheese gives these pancakes a delicate flavor and added protein.
Set up a topping bar with fresh berries, granola crumbles, honey, and/or syrup.

EASY STRAWBERRY SAUCE
1 quart fresh strawberries
1/2 cup sugar
2 tablespoons lemon juice

GRIDDLE CAKES
3 eggs
1/2 cup all-purpose flour
1 cup small curd cottage cheese
2 tablespoons butter, melted

For the sauce, rinse and trim the strawberries. Process the strawberries in a food processor until coarsely chopped or to the desired consistency. Combine with the sugar and lemon juice in a large saucepan. Cook over medium heat for 10 minutes or until thickened and bubbles cover the entire surface, stirring frequently. Spoon into a glass container or jar. Cool to room temperature before serving or storing in the refrigerator.

For the griddle cakes, beat the eggs with a fork or whisk. Add the flour, cottage cheese and butter and mix well. Pour 1/4 cup at a time onto a hot lightly greased griddle or skillet. Cook until brown on both sides, turning once. These griddle cakes will be thinner than most pancakes. Serve with the sauce.

Yield: 4 servings

FLORIDA STRAWBERRY FESTIVAL

Held each March just outside of Tampa in Plant City, the Florida

Strawberry Festival showcases top tier musical entertainment,

local agriculture, fine arts, horticulture, and livestock. Of course,

the real stars of the festival are the ripe, luscious berries.

No trip to the Florida Strawberry Festival is complete without a

serving of Plant City Strawberry Shortcake.

STRAWBERRY BREAD

Picking strawberries is a fun winter activity in Tampa. This simple and delicious bread
is a great way to use fresh berries brought home from the fields or the store.

3 cups all-purpose flour	3 eggs
1 teaspoon baking soda	1 1/4 cups vegetable oil
1 teaspoon cinnamon	1 pound fresh strawberries, sliced
1 teaspoon salt	1 1/4 cups pecans (optional)
2 cups sugar	

Preheat the oven to 350 degrees. Mix the flour, baking soda, cinnamon, salt and sugar in a bowl. Make a well in the center. Add the eggs and oil and mix until moistened. Stir in the strawberries and pecans. Pour into two greased 5×7-inch loaf pans or one 9×13-inch baking pan. Bake for 1 hour. Cool on a wire rack.

Yield: 20 servings

TROPICAL ORANGE ICE

While it may seem like a dessert, this old family recipe from one of our members
is traditionally served as a side dish during the main course. Made in advance, this fruity,
frozen concoction should sit at room temperature before cutting.

1 1/2 cups sugar	3 tablespoons fresh lemon juice
3 cups water	1 teaspoon lemon zest
3 large bananas, mashed	1 tablespoon orange zest
1 1/2 cups orange juice	1 (20-ounce) can crushed pineapple

Boil the sugar and water in a saucepan until the sugar dissolves. Remove from the heat to cool. Combine the bananas, orange juice, lemon juice, lemon zest, orange zest and undrained pineapple in a bowl and mix well. Stir in the sugar syrup. Pour into a 9×13-inch pan. Freeze for a few hours. Cut into small 1- to 2-inch squares. Serve in goblets or small bowls as a side dish.

Yield: 8 to 10 servings

MAIN ATTRACTIONS

FLORIDA LOBSTER WITH LEMON BASIL BUTTER

This recipe marries the glorious velvety flavor of grilled lobster with mellow lemon butter.

1/2 cup (1 stick) butter
1 1/2 teaspoons freshly grated lemon zest
4 (6- to 8-ounce) fresh Florida lobster tails or
frozen Florida lobster tails, thawed
1/2 cup fresh basil leaves, chopped

Preheat the grill. Melt the butter in a small saucepan over very low heat. Add the lemon zest. Pour into a small bowl. Split each lobster tail into halves lengthwise using a sharp knife or kitchen shears. Brush the exposed lobster meat lightly with the lemon butter. Place lobster meat side down on a grill rack. Grill over medium heat for 2 to 3 minutes or until lightly marked. Turn and grill for 5 to 7 minutes longer or until the lobster meat is white and firm, brushing with more of the lemon butter, if desired. Remove from the grill. Stir the basil into the remaining lemon butter. Brush each lobster tail with the lemon basil butter. Serve with the remaining lemon basil butter for dipping.

Yield: 4 servings

FLORIDA LOBSTER

The spiny lobster, or rock lobster, is a crustacean found in South

Florida and the Florida Keys. Unlike Maine lobster, it has no claws,

so the tail is the only part eaten. Many Floridians make an annual

pilgrimage to the Keys to dive for this delicacy. The meat is sweet

and tender, a rich reward for a day on the water.

WEEKNIGHT SURF AND TURF

*This combination of filet and crab meat would be the perfect
main course for an elegant birthday dinner under the stars. Easy enough to make on
a weeknight and delicious on the weekends, too.*

CRAB MEAT SALAD
8 ounces lump crab meat
1 teaspoon minced green onions
1 tablespoon minced fresh cilantro
3 tablespoons crème fraîche
1 teaspoon double-concentrated tomato
paste from a tube
1/4 teaspoon Worcestershire sauce
Kosher salt and freshly ground pepper
to taste

ROASTED BEEF FILETS
AND TOMATOES
1 tablespoon olive oil
4 center-cut beef tenderloin steaks,
about 2 inches thick

1/8 teaspoon kosher salt
1/8 teaspoon freshly ground
black pepper
1 pint cherry tomatoes, rinsed and
patted dry
Extra-virgin olive oil for drizzling
Kosher salt and freshly ground pepper
to taste

ASSEMBLY
1 bunch arugula, trimmed and rinsed
1/4 cup extra-virgin olive oil
Lemon juice to taste
Freshly ground pepper to taste

For the crab salad, combine the crab meat, green onions and cilantro in a bowl. Blend the crème fraîche, tomato paste, Worcestershire sauce, salt and pepper in a bowl. Add to the crab meat mixture and stir gently to mix. Chill, covered, until serving time.

For the beef and tomatoes, preheat the oven to 450 degrees. Heat a cast-iron or ovenproof skillet over medium heat. Add 1 tablespoon olive oil. Sprinkle both sides of the beef with 1/8 teaspoon salt and 1/8 teaspoon pepper. Sear in the olive oil for 3 minutes on each side or until brown. Move the beef to the side of the skillet. Add the tomatoes and drizzle with olive oil. Sprinkle with salt and pepper to taste. Stir the tomatoes gently to coat. Roast in the oven for 7 to 8 minutes for rare, 9 to 10 minutes for medium-rare or 12 to 13 minutes for medium.

For the assembly, toss the arugula with 1/4 cup olive oil and the lemon juice in a bowl. Sprinkle with pepper. Spoon the crab salad on top of the beef. Arrange the arugula and tomatoes on the side.

Yield: 4 servings

CAJUN SHRIMP AND LEMON PASTA

Great for a busy night, the shrimp can be prepped in the morning. Tossed together with fresh lemon pasta, your meal will be on the table in no time.

CAJUN SEASONING
1 teaspoon garlic powder
1 teaspoon onion powder
1 teaspoon paprika
1 teaspoon ground black pepper
1 teaspoon kosher salt
1/2 teaspoon dried thyme leaves
1/2 teaspoon dried oregano
1/4 teaspoon ground cayenne pepper

SPICY SHRIMP
1/2 cup olive oil
1 garlic clove
2 tablespoons fresh lemon juice
2 tablespoons chopped flat-leaf parsley

1 tablespoon brown sugar
1 tablespoon reduced-sodium soy sauce
1 pound large shrimp
Kosher salt and freshly ground pepper
   to taste

LEMON PASTA
1/2 cup olive oil
2/3 cup grated Parmesan cheese
Juice of 2 lemons
3/4 teaspoon kosher salt
1/2 teaspoon freshly ground pepper
1 pound spaghetti or penne
1/3 cup fresh basil, chopped
Zest of 2 lemons

For the seasoning, combine the garlic powder, onion powder, paprika, black pepper, salt, thyme, oregano and cayenne pepper in a jar with a tight-fitting lid. Secure the lid and shake to mix well.

For the shrimp, whisk the olive oil, whole garlic clove, Cajun seasoning, lemon juice, parsley, brown sugar and soy sauce in a 9×13-inch baking dish. Peel the shrimp and devein. Rinse under cold water and pat dry. Add to the marinade and toss to coat. Marinate, covered, in the refrigerator for 1 to 12 hours. Preheat the oven to 450 degrees. Discard the garlic clove from the shrimp. Bake for 7 to 10 minutes or until the shrimp turn pink, stirring occasionally. Remove from the oven and sprinkle with salt and pepper.

For the pasta, whisk the olive oil, cheese, lemon juice, salt and pepper in a large bowl. Cook the pasta using the package directions. Drain, reserving 1/2 cup of the pasta water. Add the pasta to the lemon sauce. Add the basil and lemon zest and toss to coat, adding the reserved pasta water a few tablespoons at a time if needed for the desired consistency. Top with the shrimp and serve. You may substitute parsley for the basil and add 2 tablespoons capers.

Yield: 4 servings

SPICE-RUBBED SHRIMP KEBABS

When living in a coastal community, shrimp "on the barbie" is a grilling standard. Using a spice rub eliminates the need to marinate ahead of time and gives the shrimp a kick of flavor.

2 tablespoons fresh rosemary	1/2 teaspoon freshly ground
2 tablespoons paprika	black pepper
2 teaspoons brown sugar	1/4 teaspoon cayenne pepper
1 teaspoon dried basil	2 pounds jumbo shrimp, peeled and
1 teaspoon dried oregano	deveined with tails left on
1 teaspoon kosher salt	Olive oil
1/2 teaspoon garlic powder	3 or 4 lemons, cut into slices or quarters

Preheat the grill. Mix the rosemary, paprika, brown sugar, basil, oregano, salt, garlic powder, black pepper and cayenne pepper in a small bowl. Place the shrimp on a large baking sheet and brush each side with olive oil. Sprinkle each side with the spice mixture to coat. Thread the shrimp onto skewers, alternating piercing through the head and tail end with each shrimp and placing a lemon slice between each pair. Brush the lemons with olive oil. Repeat until all of the shrimp and lemons are used. Place the skewers on a grill rack. Grill over medium heat for 2 to 3 minutes on each side or until the shrimp are firm and turn pink. Squeeze the grilled lemons over the shrimp before serving, if desired.

Yield: 6 serving

SHRIMP SIZES

Shrimp are graded by size, but you may also see a count number displayed. The count is the number of shrimp you can expect to find in one pound of shrimp. While labeling may vary by store, some broad categories are: jumbo, less than twenty per pound; large, twenty to thirty per pound; medium, thirty to forty per pound; and small, more than forty per pound.

BERN'S TROPICAL JUMBO SHRIMP SCAMPI AND CURRY MANGO EMULSION

Bern's Steak House is a Tampa culinary landmark famed for its extensive wine list, top-notch steaks, and attention to every detail. Executive Chef Habteab Hamde shares his exotic interpretation of shrimp scampi.

CURRY MANGO EMULSION
1 vanilla bean
2 cups (4 sticks) unsalted butter
2 very ripe mangoes
1/2 cup rice vinegar
1 cup white wine
1 cup heavy cream
1 tablespoon curry powder
Kosher salt and ground white pepper
to taste

SHRIMP SCAMPI
16 jumbo shrimp, peeled and deveined
Curry powder
2 tablespoons minced shallots

1 teaspoon minced garlic
2 tablespoons grapeseed oil or canola oil
2 ounces coconut rum
1 papaya, julienned
1 mango, julienned
3 kiwifruit, cut into wedges
1 banana, sliced
24 ounces cooked noodles or
jasmine rice
1 tablespoon minced chives
1 tablespoon finely chopped red
bell pepper
1/2 cup macadamia nuts, roasted
and chopped
Salt and pepper to taste

For the curry mango emulsion, split the vanilla bean lengthwise and scrape the seeds into the butter in a bowl. Purée the mangoes and vinegar in a blender or food processor. Heat the wine in a saucepan to burn off the alcohol. Add the mango purée. Heat until the mixture is reduced by half. Add the cream. Heat until the mixture is reduced by half. Add the curry powder, salt and white pepper. Process the purée mixture with the vanilla butter in batches in a blender until emulsified, holding the top of the blender with an oven mitt to avoid burns.

For the shrimp scampi, dust the shrimp lightly with curry powder. Sauté with the shallots and garlic in the grapeseed oil in a skillet until the shrimp begin to turn pink. Add the rum, stirring to deglaze the skillet. Cook until the rum is reduced. Add the papaya, mango, kiwifruit and banana. Cook until the fruit is heated through. Add the noodles and toss lightly to coat. Add the curry mango emulsion and toss to coat. Garnish with chives, bell pepper, macadamia nuts, salt and pepper.

Yield: 4 servings

BAKED POMPANO WITH BANANA

With a mild flavor and flaky texture, many consider pompano the best tasting Gulf fish and one of the most prized catches. Banana adds a tropical touch to this easy preparation.

1/4 cup all-purpose flour	2 bananas, cut into halves lengthwise
2 teaspoons salt	1/2 cup (1 stick) butter, melted
1 teaspoon pepper	1/2 cup sweet red vermouth
4 pompano fillets (1 pound)	

Preheat the oven to 450 degrees. Mix the flour, salt and pepper on a large plate. Dredge the fish fillets in the flour mixture, shaking off any excess. Place in a single layer in a greased large baking dish. Top each fish fillet with a banana half. Pour a mixture of the butter and vermouth over the fish fillets. Bake for 10 to 20 minutes or until the fish flakes easily, basting frequently. The pompano fillets can be with or without skin. Any firm, white fish such as yellowtail snapper, trout or redfish may be substituted.

Yield: 4 servings

COOKING FISH

Measure the thickest part of the fish and allow 10 minutes per 1 inch of thickness at 400 to 450 degrees. Use the tip of a knife to check that the fish flakes easily and is opaque, but still moist. Add a few minutes cooking time if necessary. This rule applies to fish fillets and to whole fish cooked in the oven or on the grill.

GROUPER PICCATA

The tang of lemon brightens the mild flavor of crispened grouper, a classic Gulf Coast delicacy.

1 pound fresh grouper	3/4 cup white wine
1/2 cup all-purpose flour	Zest and juice of 1 lemon
Pinch of salt	1 garlic clove, minced
Pinch of pepper	1/4 cup (1/2 stick) butter
3 tablespoons olive oil	3 tablespoons capers
1 egg, beaten	Salt and pepper to taste

Preheat the oven to 350 degrees. Rinse the fish and pat dry. Mix the flour with a pinch of salt and a pinch of pepper in a shallow dish. Heat the olive oil in a nonstick skillet over medium heat. Dip the fish in the beaten egg and dredge in the flour mixture to coat. Place in the skillet. Sear for 1 to 2 minutes on each side or until golden brown. Place the fish on a baking sheet, reserving the drippings in the skillet. Bake for 5 to 7 minutes or until the fish is nearly cooked through. Add the wine, lemon zest, lemon juice and garlic to the reserved drippings in the skillet. Simmer until the mixture is reduced by half, stirring constantly. Stir in the butter and capers. Heat until the butter melts, stirring constantly. Return the fish to the skillet. Cook for 2 to 3 minutes or until the fish flakes easily. Sprinkle with salt and pepper to taste. Place the fish on two serving plates and spoon the sauce over the top.

Yield: 2 servings

TANGERINE MARINADE

This zesty marinade is perfect for firm fish like swordfish, mahi mahi, or tuna, and also complements chicken or pork. Mix 1/2 cup each of soy sauce and tangerine juice, 10 strips tangerine zest, 6 tablespoons honey, 4 garlic cloves, minced, 1/4 cup sesame oil, 2 tablespoons minced ginger, 3 scallions, chopped, and 3 strips lemon zest together. Yields enough to marinate up to 3 pounds of chicken, pork or fish.

SPICY SAUTÉED RED SNAPPER

*A quick weeknight dinner, red snapper is one of the most popular
white fish found in the Gulf of Mexico.*

1/4 cup olive oil
2 pounds red snapper
Salt and freshly ground black
pepper to taste
1/2 cup chopped fresh parsley

1/2 teaspoon dried crushed red pepper
4 cups cherry tomatoes, cut into halves
1 cup pitted kalamata olives or other
brine-cured black olives, chopped
6 garlic cloves, minced

Heat the olive oil in a large skillet over medium-high heat. Sprinkle the fish with salt and pepper. Sauté for 3 minutes on each side or until the fish is opaque in the center and flakes easily. Remove to a platter, reserving the drippings in the skillet. Cover with tented foil to keep warm.

Sauté the parsley and red pepper in the reserved pan drippings for 1 minute. Add the tomatoes, olives and garlic. Sauté for 5 to 7 minutes or until the tomatoes are soft. Sprinkle with salt and black pepper. Uncover the fish and spoon the sauce over the top. Serve with hot cooked couscous and a green salad. Tilapia or orange roughy may be used.

Yield: 4 servings

WINE AND SEAFOOD

*Crisp, white wines act like a squeeze of lemon over
seafood; they cleanse your palate and heighten appreciation of the
food's flavors. Lighter dishes call for clean, unoaked wines like
Sauvignon Blanc or Pinot Grigio. Riesling, which often has a touch
of sweetness, usually pairs well with spicy preparations.*

PLANKED SEA TROUT WITH LEMON

*While grilling on a cedar plank is often associated with the
Pacific Northwest, this Gulf Coast adaptation uses local fish for a Florida feel.
You may also use mackerel, kingfish, or amberjack.*

1 small lemon	3 tablespoons soy sauce
1 tablespoon chopped fresh dill weed	3 tablespoons chicken stock
1/2 teaspoon freshly ground pepper	3 tablespoons finely chopped green
2 garlic cloves, crushed	onions (white and green portions)
2 tablespoons brown sugar	1 (1 1/2-pound) sea trout fillet
3 tablespoons canola oil	

Soak a cedar plank large enough to hold the fish in cool water to cover for 1 to 2 hours, weighting to submerge if necessary. Rinse the lemon well. Cut a 1-inch wide by 5- or 6-inch-long piece of zest from one end of the lemon with a vegetable peeler. Cut the remaining lemon into two or three thin slices. Mix the lemon zest, dill weed, pepper, garlic, brown sugar, canola oil, soy sauce, stock and green onions in a 1-gallon sealable plastic bag. Add the fish and marinate in the refrigerator for 1 to 3 hours, turning once or twice.

Preheat the grill to 400 degrees. Drain the fish, discarding the marinade. Place the fish skin side down on the soaked cedar plank. Place the lemon slices over the fish. Place the plank in the center of a grill rack. Grill, covered, over medium-high heat for 15 to 20 minutes or until the edges of the fish are brown and the fish is cooked through. Remove the plank with the fish from the grill and let stand for 5 minutes. To serve, cut into pieces and lift the pieces off the skin with a spatula.

Yield: 4 servings

PECAN-CRUSTED TILAPIA WITH BLUEBERRY-BALSAMIC REDUCTION

Tilapia is a popular farm-raised fish, but this South American native also has found a home in our lakes and rivers. This mild-flavored white fish is paired with a simple but flavorful sauce using local blueberries for a sweet-and-savory treat.

BLUEBERRY-BALSAMIC REDUCTION
1 cup blueberries
1/4 cup balsamic vinegar
Salt to taste
Sugar to taste

PECAN-CRUSTED TILAPIA
1 cup pecans
1/2 cup all-purpose flour
1 egg
1/2 cup all-purpose flour
4 tilapia fillets
2 tablespoons unsalted butter
Canola oil or grapeseed oil

For the reduction, cook three-fourths of the blueberries and the vinegar in a small saucepan over medium heat until reduced by half. Remove from the heat to cool. Purée in a blender. Add salt and sugar if needed to bring out the flavors. Return to the saucepan. Add the remaining blueberries. Cook until heated through.

For the fish, preheat the oven to 350 degrees. Pulse the pecans in a food processor to form a coarse meal. Mix the pecan meal with 1/2 cup flour in a shallow dish. Beat the egg in a shallow dish. Place 1/2 cup flour in another shallow dish. Dredge the fish in the flour. Dip in the egg and then dredge in the pecan mixture to coat. Melt the butter in a large skillet. Add enough canola oil to the skillet to fill 1/4 inch deep. Fry the fish for 2 to 4 minutes on both sides or until golden brown. Remove to paper towels to drain. Place the fish on a baking sheet. Bake for 5 to 7 minutes. Place the fish on serving plates and spoon the reduction over the top.

Yield: 4 servings

MOJO BEEF KEBABS

*Mojo is a signature Cuban marinade that can be used for beef, pork,
fish, and chicken. While variations of this staple sauce abound, the key element is the
sour orange that grows throughout Cuba and Florida.*

1/3 cup orange juice	2 garlic cloves
1/3 cup fresh lime juice	Salt and pepper to taste
Zest of 1 lime	1 1/2 to 2 pounds boneless sirloin,
3 tablespoons chopped fresh oregano	cut into 1 1/2-inch cubes
3 tablespoons olive oil	1 lime, cut into wedges
3 tablespoons chopped fresh parsley	1 small red onion, cut into chunks
2 teaspoons ground cumin	1 pint grape tomatoes

Process the orange juice, lime juice, lime zest, oregano, olive oil, parsley, cumin, garlic, salt and
pepper in a food processor until blended. Reserve half the sauce. Place the beef and the remaining sauce in
a sealable plastic bag and marinate in the refrigerator for 30 to 60 minutes. Soak wooden skewers in water
to cover in a shallow dish for 30 to 60 minutes.

Preheat the grill. Drain the beef, discarding the marinade. Thread the beef, lime wedges, onion
and tomatoes alternately onto the wooden skewers. Grill for 10 minutes, turning several times. Serve
drizzled with the reserved sauce.

Yield: 6 to 8 servings

SUMMER REDS

*Think it's too hot to drink red wine? Think again. While
we talk about red wines being served at room temperature, most reds
taste better served at 60 to 65 degrees Fahrenheit. Chilling them in
the refrigerator for 10 to 15 minutes usually does the trick. Lighter
reds with little tannin can be served even cooler. On a warm
evening, try putting a Beaujolais or pinot noir in a Champagne
bucket full of ice and water for 15 to 20 minutes.*

PASTITSIO

A bewitching blend of flavors, this classic Greek dish updates the
Pastitsio recipe in The Gasparilla Cookbook.

PASTA
8 ounces ground sirloin
4 ounces ground pork
4 ounces ground lamb
1 cup chopped onion
1 tablespoon chopped fresh parsley
1/2 teaspoon cinnamon
1 teaspoon kosher salt
1/2 teaspoon freshly ground pepper
1 (14-ounce) can whole tomatoes
1 (8-ounce) can tomato sauce
2 or 3 sprigs of fresh thyme
16 ounces ziti
1 tablespoon butter or vegetable oil

BÉCHAMEL SAUCE
2 tablespoons unsalted butter
2 tablespoons all-purpose flour
2 cups milk
2 egg yolks, lightly beaten
2 tablespoons grated Parmesan cheese
Pinch of nutmeg
1/2 teaspoon kosher salt

ASSEMBLY
2 tablespoons grated Parmesan cheese

For the pasta, brown the sirloin, pork and lamb in a skillet over medium-high heat, stirring until crumbly. Add the onion, parsley, cinnamon, 1 teaspoon salt and the pepper. Cook until the onion is translucent, stirring constantly. Add the tomatoes and stir with a spoon to break up. Stir in the tomato sauce. Add the thyme. Simmer, covered, over low heat for 40 minutes. Cook the pasta using the package directions. Drain the pasta and return to the pan. Add the butter and toss to coat. Cover and set aside. Adjust the seasonings in the meat sauce. Discard the thyme. Add the meat sauce to the pasta and toss to coat.

For the béchamel sauce, melt the butter in a small saucepan over medium heat. Add the flour and mix well. Cook over medium heat for 2 to 3 minutes or until pale brown. Add the milk gradually, stirring constantly to prevent lumps. Heat just to the boiling point. Reduce the heat to low. Simmer until slightly thickened, stirring frequently. Remove from the heat. Whisk the egg yolks in a heatproof bowl. Whisk 2 teaspoons of the hot milk mixture into the egg yolks. Pour the remaining hot milk mixture into the egg yolks carefully, whisking until smooth. Stir in the cheese, nutmeg and salt.

For the assembly, preheat the oven to 325 degrees. Spread the pasta mixture in a large deep baking dish. Pour the béchamel sauce over the pasta. Sprinkle with the cheese. Bake for 45 minutes or until the top is golden brown.

Yield: 8 to 10 servings

PICADILLO

This terrific dish showcases the Cuban heritage in our community.
Try it served with black beans and a side of Cuban bread from La Segunda
Central Bakery, a Tampa institution since 1915.

3/4 cup chopped yellow onion
3/4 cup chopped green bell pepper
1 1/2 tablespoons minced garlic
2 tablespoons extra-virgin olive oil
1 pound ground beef
1 (8-ounce) can tomato sauce
1 teaspoon oregano

1/4 teaspoon garlic powder
1/4 teaspoon onion powder
1/2 teaspoon kosher salt
8 Spanish green olives, finely chopped
2 tablespoons raisins (optional)
2 tablespoons red wine vinegar
Hot cooked white rice

Sauté the onion, bell pepper and garlic in the olive oil in a large skillet over medium-high heat. Cook for 3 to 5 minutes or until the onion is translucent. Add the ground beef. Cook until the ground beef is brown, stirring until crumbly. Drain the ground beef mixture and return to the skillet. Reduce the heat to low. Add the tomato sauce, oregano, garlic powder, onion powder, salt, olives and raisins and mix well. Stir in the vinegar. Simmer, covered, for 20 minutes. Serve over hot white rice. This recipe can also be wrapped in pastry and fried to make empanadas.

Yield: 4 servings

CUBAN BREAD

What is one yard long, crusty on the outside, fluffy

white on the inside, and baked with a palm frond on top? It's Cuban

bread, of course. Freshly baked in Tampa's Ybor City,

Cuban bread is the basis for the ever-popular Cuban sandwich and

is simply divine toasted, slathered with butter, and served

hot with your favorite Cuban fare.

GUAVA-GLAZED PORK TENDERLOIN

*The distinctive sweetness of guava gives a Tampa touch to this simple
yet elegant dinner party entrée.*

1/3 cup guava jelly
2 teaspoons Dijon mustard
2 tablespoons orange juice
1 teaspoon ground cumin
1 teaspoon kosher salt
1/2 teaspoon freshly ground pepper
1 (12- to 16-ounce) pork tenderloin
1 tablespoon butter
2 teaspoons cider vinegar

Melt the jelly, Dijon mustard and orange juice in a small saucepan. Remove from the heat. Cover with foil to keep warm. Mix the cumin, salt and pepper together. Rub over the pork. Cook the pork in the butter in a skillet over medium-high heat for 8 minutes or until brown. Reduce the heat to medium-low. Cook, covered, for 10 to 20 minutes or to 160 degrees on a meat thermometer inserted in the thickest portion, turning every 4 to 5 minutes.

Remove the pork to a platter to rest, reserving the drippings in the skillet. Add the vinegar to the reserved drippings. Cook over medium heat, stirring to scrape up any brown bits from the bottom of the skillet. Reduce the heat to low. Add the jelly mixture and mix well. Return the pork and any accumulated juices to the skillet, turning to coat. Place the pork on a cutting board. Adjust the seasoning of the glaze, if desired. Cut the pork crosswise into slices 1/2 inch thick. Drizzle the pork slices with the glaze and serve.

Yield: 3 to 4 servings

LEMON-HERB ROASTED CHICKEN

A dry rub of seasoned salt gives similar results to brining
without the mess. Be sure to allow time for the salt to do its job, and you will
have a moist and flavorful roasted chicken.

1 (3½- to 5-pound) chicken
2 tablespoons kosher salt
2 tablespoons chopped fresh thyme or
sage, or a mixture of both
2 teaspoons lemon zest
1 teaspoon ground coriander

½ teaspoon garlic powder
½ teaspoon freshly ground pepper
½ lemon
3 or 4 garlic cloves, crushed
1 tablespoon unsalted butter, melted

Remove the giblet bag from the chicken cavity. Trim any excess fat. Place breast side up on a rack in a shallow 10×15-inch roasting pan. Mix the salt, thyme, lemon zest, coriander, garlic powder and pepper together. Rub over the chicken and into the creases to coat evenly. Chill, uncovered, for 6 to 10 hours.

Preheat the oven to 400 degrees. Place the lemon and garlic in the chicken cavity. Brush with the butter. Roast for 1 hour or to 170 degrees on a meat thermometer when inserted into the thickest portion of the thigh, basting every 15 to 20 minutes with additional butter or with the pan drippings. Remove to a cutting board. Let stand for 10 minutes before carving.

Yield: 3 to 6 servings

STYLES OF WHITE WINE

White wines can be broadly divided into "oaked" and
"unoaked" wines, based on whether the wine was aged in wooden
barrels. Oak-aging, commonly used for chardonnay and fumé blanc,
gives a buttery flavor and a rich mouth-feel to the wine. Oaked wines
typically pair well with salmon, chicken, and pork dishes.

GRECIAN CHICKEN BREASTS

*Spinach and feta cheese give this dish its traditional Greek flavor.
A great "make-ahead" for a quick weeknight meal. When paired with yellow rice and a
green salad, this is a modern-day classic.*

6 boneless chicken breasts
Salt and pepper to taste
1 (10-ounce) package frozen chopped
spinach, thawed and drained
8 ounces water-pack feta cheese, drained and chopped
1/2 cup mayonnaise
1 garlic clove, minced
12 slices bacon

Preheat the oven to 350 degrees. Trim the chicken of any excess fat. Cut a pocket horizontally in each. Sprinkle with salt and pepper. Squeeze any excess liquid from the spinach. Combine the spinach, cheese, mayonnaise, garlic, salt and pepper in a medium bowl and mix well. Stuff into each chicken breast. Wrap each tightly with two bacon slices to enclose the filling. Place on a rack in a baking pan. Bake for 35 to 40 minutes or until cooked through. To prepare in advance, wrap in foil and chill or freeze until ready to bake. If frozen, thaw before baking. For a creamy side dish, double the stuffing, place the remaining stuffing in individual ramekins and bake with the chicken.

Yield: 6 servings

CHICKEN KEBABS

*Fresh orange and lime juice with a zing of fresh ginger create big
flavor for this simple kebab. Marinate the chicken in the morning and assemble your
kebabs before guests arrive to enjoy a stress-free get-together.*

1 cup soy sauce	1 red bell pepper, cut into
1/4 cup fresh orange juice	1-inch pieces
1/4 cup fresh lime juice	1 green bell pepper, cut into
1 teaspoon grated fresh ginger	1-inch pieces
1 teaspoon minced garlic	1 red onion, cut into 1-inch pieces
2 pounds boneless skinless chicken	
breasts, cut into 1-inch pieces	

Mix the soy sauce, orange juice, lime juice, ginger and garlic in a medium bowl. Add the chicken. Marinate in the refrigerator for 3 to 6 hours. Soak wooden skewers in water to cover in a shallow dish while the chicken marinates.

Preheat the grill. Drain the chicken, discarding the marinade. Thread the chicken, bell peppers and onion alternately onto the skewers. Place on a grill rack. Grill until the chicken is cooked through but still moist.

Yield: 4 to 6 servings

GINGER

*It's easy to always have fresh ginger on hand. Peel the
ginger and store in a sealable plastic bag in the freezer. Grate as
needed—there is no need to defrost.*

CHICKEN SOUVLAKI

Souvlaki is a Greek specialty consisting of marinated beef, pork, or chicken usually cut into pieces, grilled on skewers, and served with tzatziki sauce on pita bread. Serve the tzatziki sauce with pita chips for a tasty starter.

CHICKEN
2 tablespoons extra-virgin olive oil
1 tablespoon fresh lemon juice
1 tablespoon balsamic vinegar
1 teaspoon dried oregano
1/2 teaspoon garlic powder
1/2 teaspoon kosher salt
Freshly ground pepper to taste
1 1/2 to 2 pounds boneless skinless chicken breasts

TZATZIKI SAUCE
1 cucumber, peeled and shredded
1/2 teaspoon kosher salt
1 (7-ounce) package strained Greek whole milk yogurt
1 tablespoon fresh lemon juice
1/2 teaspoon minced garlic
2 tablespoons finely chopped fresh dill weed
Kosher salt and freshly ground pepper to taste

SANDWICH
1 (5-count) package Mediterranean flat bread rounds
2 to 3 cups shredded romaine
1 to 2 cups chopped tomatoes or grape tomato halves
Thinly sliced red onion to taste
Pitted kalamata olive slices to taste
Pepperoncini rounds to taste
Crumbled feta cheese to taste

For the chicken, mix the olive oil, lemon juice, vinegar, oregano, garlic powder, salt and pepper in a shallow dish or a sealable plastic bag. Add the chicken, turning to coat. Marinate in the refrigerator for 1 hour or longer. Preheat the grill. Drain the chicken, discarding the marinade. Grill the chicken over high heat to 170 degrees on a meat thermometer. Let stand for 10 minutes. Cut crosswise into strips. The chicken may be broiled for 8 to 10 minutes on each side or until cooked through.

For the tzatziki sauce, toss the cucumber with 1/2 teaspoon salt in a colander or large sieve placed over a bowl. Drain for 15 to 30 minutes. Squeeze any excess liquid from the cucumber and place in a bowl. Add the yogurt, lemon juice, garlic, dill weed and salt and pepper to taste and mix well. Chill, covered, until serving time.

For the sandwich, preheat the grill. Grill the bread for 1 minute on each side to warm. Spread the bread with some of the tzatziki sauce. Layer the chicken, romaine and tomatoes over the bread. Top with the remaining tzatziki sauce, onion, olives, pepperoncini and cheese and fold in half lengthwise.

Yield: 4 servings

ANTIPASTI SANDWICH

This sandwich is better the longer the ingredients meld together,
making it ideal for a day at the beach or on the boat.

1 loaf focaccia	4 slices provolone cheese
2 or 3 tablespoons Dijon mustard	2 cups arugula
8 ounces sliced deli ham or turkey	1 tablespoon olive oil
3 Roasted Red Bell Peppers,	2 teaspoons balsamic vinegar
cut into strips (page 52)	Salt and pepper to taste

Cut the bread into halves horizontally. Spread the Dijon mustard in a thin layer on the cut sides of the bread. Layer the ham and roasted bell peppers on one of the bread halves. Layer the cheese on the remaining bread half. Toss the arugula with the olive oil, vinegar, salt and pepper in a bowl. Pile on top of the ham and roasted bell peppers. Place the remaining bread half cheese side down on top of the arugula. Press firmly and cut into four equal pieces.

Place the sandwich on a layer of plastic wrap, keeping all four pieces together, and wrap tightly. Store in the refrigerator or a cooler until serving time. The longer the sandwich is stored, the better the flavors of the sandwich will meld.

Yield: 4 servings

STORING TOMATOES

For the best flavor and texture, never refrigerate a

tomato. Keep out of direct sunlight, and store stem side up

to prevent bruised shoulders.

CAPRESE SANDWICH WITH FRESH PESTO

A hearty take-along sandwich makes great use of perfectly ripe local tomatoes.
Serve the pesto on pasta by simply adding an additional 1/4 cup olive oil.

FRESH PESTO
1 cup fresh basil leaves, loosely packed
1/2 cup walnuts, chopped
2 garlic cloves
1/2 cup (2 ounces) grated
   Parmesan cheese
1/4 teaspoon kosher salt
1/4 cup olive oil

SANDWICH
1 (8- to 10-inch) round foccacia or
   French baguette
1 to 2 tablespoons mayonnaise
8 ounces mozzarella cheese,
   thinly sliced
1 avocado, thinly sliced
2 cups field green salad mix
1 large tomato, thinly sliced
Salt and pepper to taste

For the pesto, process the basil, walnuts, garlic, cheese, salt and olive oil in a food processor until smooth or to the desired consistency, stopping to scrape down the side of the bowl occasionally. Remove to a bowl. Cover the surface of the pesto with plastic wrap. Chill until serving time.

For the sandwich, cut the bread into halves horizontally. Cover the top half with the pesto. Spread the bottom half with the mayonnaise. Layer the mayonnaise half with the cheese, avocado, salad mix and tomato. Sprinkle with salt and pepper. Replace the top half pesto side down and press gently to adhere. Wrap tightly in plastic wrap or baking parchment. Chill until serving time. To serve, unwrap and cut into quarters, securing with wooden picks, if desired.

Yield: 2 to 4 servings

CAPTURE THE COAST

TEMPTATIONS

CULINARY COLLECTION

FLORIDA KEY LIME PIE WITH GINGERSNAP CRUST

A Tampa native shared this incredible, decades-old recipe for this iconic Florida dessert. No trip to the Sunshine State is complete without a slice.

1 1/2 cups crumbled gingersnap cookies
3/4 cup sweetened flaked coconut
1/4 cup (1/2 stick) unsalted
butter, melted
1 (14-ounce) can sweetened
condensed milk

1/2 cup Key lime juice
1 teaspoon lime zest
4 egg yolks
Whipped cream
Toasted sweetened flaked coconut

Preheat the oven to 350 degrees. Pulse the cookies in a food processor until finely ground. Add 3/4 cup coconut and pulse to mix. Add the butter and pulse to mix. Press over the bottom and up the side of a 9-inch pie plate. Bake for 8 to 10 minutes or until golden brown. Cool on a wire rack. Maintain the oven temperature. For a nuttier flavor, toast the coconut.

Combine the condensed milk, lime juice, lime zest and egg yolks in a bowl and beat well. Pour into the cooled crust. Bake for 7 to 10 minutes or until set. Let stand until cool. Top each slice with a dollop of whipped cream and sprinkle with toasted coconut. The pie also may be made using a graham cracker crust.

Yield: 8 to 10 servings

PREPARING A CAKE MIX

Sifting a cake mix before using it adds air to the batter, which

will make the cake lighter and fluffier after baking.

GOLDEN AMARETTO CAKE WITH FRESH STRAWBERRIES

Fresh strawberries are a wonderful addition to this light moist cake. You will find yourself coming back to this recipe again and again.

1 (2-layer) package yellow cake mix	1/4 teaspoon almond extract
1 (6-ounce) package vanilla instant pudding mix	12 tablespoons amaretto, divided
1/2 cup vegetable oil	2 cups confectioners' sugar, divided
4 eggs	16 ounces strawberries, thinly sliced
3/4 cup water	1 tablespoon granulated sugar

Preheat the oven to 350 degrees. Beat the cake mix, pudding mix, oil, eggs, water and almond extract in a mixing bowl until smooth. Pour into a lightly greased and floured bundt pan. Bake for 45 to 50 minutes or until the cake springs back when lightly touched. Mix 6 tablespoons of the amaretto and 1 cup of the confectioners' sugar in a bowl. Pierce several holes in the warm cake with a fork or skewer. Pour the amaretto mixture over the cake, allowing to absorb evenly. Cool in the pan for 2 hours or longer. Invert onto a cake plate.

Mix the remaining amaretto and confectioners' sugar in a bowl. Drizzle over the top of the cake, allowing the glaze to run down the side. Toss the strawberries with the granulated sugar in a bowl. Let stand for 20 to 30 minutes before serving. Cut the cake into slices and top with the strawberries. The cake may be baked in small bundt pans for individual servings.

Yield: 12 servings

HUMMINGBIRD CAKE WITH CREAM CHEESE FROSTING

Fall in love with this Southern standard. The tropical flavors of pineapple and banana topped with lush cream cheese frosting will leave you yearning for another slice.

CAKE
3 cups all-purpose flour
2 cups sugar
1/2 teaspoon salt
2 teaspoons baking soda
1 teaspoon cinnamon
3 eggs, beaten
1 1/4 cups vegetable oil
2 teaspoons vanilla extract
1 (8-ounce) can crushed pineapple
1 cup pecans, chopped
2 cups mashed bananas
2 tablespoons brown sugar

CREAM CHEESE FROSTING
16 ounces cream cheese, softened
1 cup (2 sticks) unsalted butter, softened
2 teaspoons vanilla extract
1 (2-pound) package confectioners' sugar

ASSEMBLY
Pecan pieces

For the cake, preheat the oven to 350 degrees. Sift the flour, sugar, salt, baking soda and cinnamon three times into a mixing bowl. Add the eggs and oil and stir with a wooden spoon until the ingredients are moistened. Add the vanilla, pineapple and pecans and mix well. Add the bananas and brown sugar and mix well. Divide evenly among three greased and floured 8- or 9-inch cake pans. Bake for 25 to 35 minutes or until a wooden pick inserted into the centers of the layers come out clean. Cool in the pans for 15 minutes. Invert onto a wire rack to cool completely.

For the frosting, beat the cream cheese and butter in a mixing bowl until smooth and creamy. Stir in the vanilla. Sift in the confectioners' sugar 2 cups at a time, beating well after each addition.

To assemble, spread the frosting between the layers and over the top and side of the cake. Decorate with pecans.

Yield: 12 servings

CARAMEL CREAM CAKE

A beautiful addition to any dessert buffet, the velvety caramel frosting
on this three-layer cake is simply sublime.

CAKE
$2^2/3$ cups all-purpose flour
$1/4$ teaspoon baking soda
1 teaspoon salt
1 cup (2 sticks) butter, softened
3 cups sugar
6 eggs
1 cup sour cream
1 tablespoon vanilla extract

CARAMEL FROSTING
1 cup (2 sticks) butter
2 cups light brown sugar
$1/2$ cup evaporated milk
$1/2$ teaspoon vanilla extract
4 cups confectioners' sugar

For the cake, preheat the oven to 350 degrees. Sift the flour, baking soda and salt together. Cream the butter and sugar in a mixing bowl until light and fluffy. Add the eggs one at a time, beating well after each addition. Add the flour mixture and sour cream alternately, beating constantly. Stir in the vanilla. Pour into three greased and floured cake pans. Bake for 25 to 35 minutes or until the layers test done. Cool in the pans on a wire rack for 10 minutes. Invert onto a wire rack to cool completely.

For the frosting, melt the butter in a saucepan. Stir in the brown sugar and evaporated milk. Cook for 2 minutes over medium heat, stirring constantly. Remove from the heat. Stir in the vanilla. Pour over the confectioners' sugar in a bowl and beat until smooth. Cool slightly. Spread between the layers and over the top and side of the cake.

Yield: 12 servings

LEMON CREAM SPONGE CAKE

This elegant dessert uses a sponge cake that gets its lightness from beaten egg whites, and the luscious lemon cream filling is a soothing complement to the airy cake.

LEMON CREAM FILLING
2 1/2 tablespoons cornstarch
1/4 cup cold water
1 cup milk
1/2 cup sugar
2 teaspoons grated lemon zest
1/4 cup lemon juice
2 egg yolks, lightly beaten
1/2 cup heavy whipping cream, chilled

CAKE
1 cup all-purpose flour
1 1/2 teaspoons baking powder
4 egg whites, at room temperature
3/4 cup sugar
4 egg yolks
1 teaspoon unsalted butter, melted
1/3 cup milk

ASSEMBLY
1 cup heavy whipping cream, chilled
1 tablespoon confectioners' sugar

For the lemon filling, whisk the cornstarch into the water in a small saucepan until smooth. Add the milk and sugar. Cook over low heat until the mixture boils and thickens. Remove from the heat. Stir in the lemon zest and lemon juice. Whisk 1 to 2 teaspoons of the hot milk mixture into the egg yolks. Whisk the egg yolks into the hot milk mixture. Cook over low heat for 2 minutes, stirring constantly. Cool to room temperature. Beat the whipping cream in a mixing bowl until firm peaks form. Fold into the lemon custard; chill.

For the cake, preheat the oven to 350 degrees. Line the bottom of an 8-inch cake pan with baking parchment. Cut a 4×25-inch piece of baking parchment and line the side of the prepared pan. The baking parchment should stand 2 inches above the top of the cake pan and the ends should overlap to create a tall tube. Spray the baking parchment with nonstick cooking spray. Sift the flour and baking powder together. Beat the egg whites in a mixing bowl until glossy, soft peaks form. Add the sugar gradually, beating until stiff peaks form. Beat in the egg yolks. Fold in the flour mixture. Fold in the butter and milk. Spoon carefully into the prepared cake pan. Adjust the baking parchment if needed to keep the tube standing tall and straight. Bake for 25 to 30 minutes or until light brown and a cake tester comes out clean. Cool for 1 hour or to room temperature.

For the assembly, cut the cake horizontally into four even layers. Spread the lemon filling between the cake layers, using about 1/3 to 1/2 cup between each layer. Beat the whipping cream with the sugar in a mixing bowl until firm peaks form. Spread over the top and side of the cake. Chill for several hours before serving.

Yield: 8 servings

LEMON CAKE WITH MIXED BERRY SAUCE

*One of our testers referred to this lemony confection
as "bikini-ready" due to its light preparation.*

CAKE
1¹/₂ cups sifted cake flour
1 cup sugar
1¹/₂ teaspoons baking powder
¹/₂ teaspoon salt
¹/₂ cup fresh lemon juice
2¹/₂ tablespoons lemon zest
5 tablespoons canola oil
1¹/₂ teaspoons vanilla extract
3 egg yolks
8 egg whites, at room temperature

³/₄ teaspoon cream of tartar
2 tablespoons sugar

MIXED BERRY SAUCE
1 (12-ounce) package frozen
   mixed berries
6 tablespoons water
³/₄ cup sugar
4 teaspoons fresh lemon juice
1 (12-ounce) package frozen
   mixed berries

For the cake, preheat the oven to 325 degrees. Whisk the cake flour, 1 cup sugar, the baking powder and salt in a large bowl. Whisk the lemon juice, lemon zest, canola oil, vanilla and egg yolks in a medium bowl. Add to the cake flour mixture and stir until smooth. Beat the egg whites in a large bowl until foamy. Add the cream of tartar and beat until soft peaks form. Add 2 tablespoons sugar gradually, beating until stiff peaks form. Fold one-fourth of the egg white mixture into the batter. Fold in the remaining egg white mixture. Spoon into an ungreased 10-inch tube pan, spreading evenly. Bake for 45 minutes or until the cake springs back when lightly touched. Invert the pan and let stand until cool. Loosen the cake from the side of the cake pan with a knife. Invert onto a cake plate.

For the sauce, combine 1 package berries, the water, sugar and lemon juice in a saucepan. Cook over medium heat for 10 minutes. Add 1 package berries. Cook for 8 minutes longer, stirring frequently. Cut the cake into slices and serve with the warm sauce.

Yield: 12 servings

STRAWBERRY SHORTCAKE WITH SWEET CREAM BISCUITS

If you can't visit Plant City during the annual Strawberry Festival in February, you can bring home the heavenly flavors with this presentation of the classic shortcake.

STRAWBERRIES
2 cups strawberries
1/4 cup sugar

BALSAMIC REDUCTION
2 tablespoons balsamic vinegar
2 tablespoons sugar

SWEET CREAM BISCUITS
2 cups all-purpose flour
1/3 cup sugar
2 1/2 teaspoons baking powder
1/2 teaspoon salt
1 1/2 cups heavy cream

ASSEMBLY
Whipped cream

For the strawberries, rinse the strawberries. Cut into slices and place in a bowl. Sprinkle with the sugar and stir to coat. Chill, covered with plastic wrap, for 30 minutes or longer before serving. The strawberries will make their own syrup as they chill.

For the reduction, bring the vinegar and sugar to a simmer in a small saucepan. Cook until the mixture is reduced by half.

For the biscuits, preheat the oven to 450 degrees. Mix the flour, sugar, baking powder and salt in a large bowl. Stir in the cream gradually. Continue to mix with floured hands until well mixed. Place on a lightly floured surface and roll 1 inch thick. Cut with a 2- or 3-inch biscuit cutter. Place on an ungreased baking sheet. Bake for 10 to 12 minutes or until light brown.

For the assembly, place two biscuits on each serving plate. Top with the strawberries and drizzle with the reduction. Garnish with whipped cream.

Yield: 6 to 8 servings

CHOCOLATE TART

A rich, elegant dessert for a dinner party. Make this earlier in the day and
serve chilled with a dollop of freshly whipped cream.

TART CRUST	CHOCOLATE GANACHE FILLING
1/2 cup (1 stick) chilled unsalted butter	1/2 cup (3 ounces) bittersweet chocolate
2 cups all-purpose flour	chips (at least 60 percent cacao)
1/4 teaspoon salt	1 cup (6 ounces) semisweet
1/3 cup sugar	chocolate chips
2 teaspoons fresh lemon juice	1 1/2 cups half-and-half
2 eggs	2 eggs

For the crust, cut the butter into 1/2-inch pieces. Pulse the butter, flour, salt and sugar in a food processor fitted with a cutting blade for 10 seconds or until no large pieces of butter remain. Add the lemon juice and eggs. Pulse briefly until the dough begins to form a ball. Place on a large square of plastic wrap and shape into a ball. Sprinkle the entire surface with flour and wrap tightly in the plastic wrap, twisting the corners together. Place seam side down in a bowl. Chill for 30 minutes. Preheat the oven to 350 degrees. Unwrap the dough and place on a lightly floured surface. Roll with a lightly floured rolling pin into a 12-inch circle. If the dough is sticky or is hard to work with, roll between a sheet of waxed paper and the plastic wrap. Fit the circle in an 11-inch tart pan with a removable bottom, folding any excess dough under to reinforce the rim. Top with a piece of baking parchment and fill with pie weights or dried beans or rice. Bake for 18 minutes. Remove from the oven and set aside. Maintain the oven temperature.

For the filling, place the chocolate chips and half-and-half in a microwave-safe bowl. Microwave at 50 percent power for 3 minutes, stirring after each minute. Stir to mix well. The chocolate should be melted and smooth. If not, microwave for 1 minute longer at 50 percent power. Beat the eggs in a mixing bowl for 1 to 2 minutes or until pale yellow. Fold in the chocolate mixture. Beat for 1 minute or until smooth.

For the assembly, pour the filling into the warm tart crust. The crust will be very full. Bake for 25 minutes or just until the filling is set. Remove from the oven and cool on a wire rack to room temperature. The filling will become firm as it cools. Chill until serving time. Serve cool or at room temperature with whipped cream or sliced fresh strawberries.

Yield: 10 to 12 servings

COLUMBIA RESTAURANT'S FLAN

A true Ybor City classic, the Columbia Restaurant's Flan de Leche was previously featured in The Gasparilla Cookbook *and in* Tampa Treasures. *The recipe was recently updated and the Gonzmarts have generously shared the new version with us.*

1 cup sweetened condensed milk
1 cup evaporated milk
3/4 cup whole milk
3 eggs
1 1/4 teaspoons vanilla extract
1 cup sugar
1 tablespoon water

Preheat the oven to 400 degrees. Combine the condensed milk, evaporated milk, whole milk, eggs and vanilla in a bowl and mix well. Cook the sugar and water in a saucepan over medium heat until golden, stirring constantly. Pour immediately into six custard cups. Top with the milk mixture. Place the cups in a large baking pan and place in the hot oven. Fill the larger pan with hot water. Bake for 30 minutes. Do not let the water boil. Add a few ice cubes if necessary to prevent boiling. Carefully remove the cups from the water bath. Chill in the refrigerator. To serve, unmold by pressing the edges of the custard with a spoon to break away from the cup and invert onto a serving plate. Spoon the caramelized sugar from the bottom over the top of each custard.

Yield: 6 servings

CANNOLI

Store-bought cannoli shells make this classic Italian pastry a cinch. Layer the cannoli filling in a trifle dish with ladyfingers and top with chocolate shavings for an elegant dessert.

32 ounces soft whole milk
ricotta cheese
1 tablespoon vanilla extract
1 cup confectioners' sugar, sifted
1/2 teaspoon cinnamon

1 cup pecans, finely chopped
1 cup miniature chocolate
chips, divided
12 cannoli shells, or 24 miniature
cannoli shells

Combine the cheese, vanilla, confectioners' sugar and cinnamon in a mixing bowl and mix well. Stir in the pecans and 1/4 cup of the chocolate chips. Chill for 2 hours or longer before serving. Place the filling in a pastry bag or in a plastic bag with the corner snipped off. Pipe the filling into the cannoli shells. Place the remaining chocolate chips in a small bowl. Dip the ends of each cannoli into the chocolate chips to coat. For additional garnishes, try colored jimmies, chopped nuts or chopped maraschino cherries. Also try dipping the edges of the shells into melted chocolate before filling.

Yield: 12 servings

MACERATED ORANGE SECTIONS

Cut off the tops of 4 large navel oranges to expose the flesh. Cut the peel away from the sides and remove all the white pith. Free the sections from the core of the orange and place in a bowl. When all of the sections have been removed, squeeze the orange core over a measuring cup to extract the remaining juice. Blend 1/4 cup orange juice, 1/2 cup Mint Simple Syrup (page 28) and 4 teaspoons grenadine in a bowl. Pour over the orange sections. Chill until serving time. Spoon into serving bowls and top with a scoop of vanilla ice cream.

TAMPA'S BAKLAVA

*Stop into one of the many Greek bakeries lining the sponge
docks in Tarpon Springs, and you will find this classic pastry. Our version uses pecans,
a delightful substitute for the usual walnuts.*

1/2 cup honey	8 ounces finely chopped pecans
1/2 cup sugar	or walnuts
1/3 cup water	1 teaspoon cinnamon
1 teaspoon lemon juice	1/4 teaspoon salt
1 teaspoon cinnamon	1/2 cup (1 stick) butter
1/2 teaspoon ground cloves (optional)	1 (16-ounce) package phyllo dough,
	thawed

Combine the honey, sugar, water, lemon juice, 1 teaspoon cinnamon and the cloves in a medium saucepan and mix well. Cook over medium heat until all of the ingredients are dissolved, stirring constantly. Reduce the heat to low. Cook for 10 minutes. Remove from the heat to cool.

Preheat the oven to 350 degrees. Mix the pecans, 1 teaspoon cinnamon and the salt in a bowl. Melt the butter in a small saucepan over low heat. Unroll the phyllo dough and cut into 8×8-inch sheets. Cover with waxed paper topped with a damp towel. Keep the unused portion covered until needed.

Layer eight sheets of the phyllo dough in a greased 8×8-inch baking pan, brushing each sheet with butter. Sprinkle one-fourth of the pecan mixture over the top. Cover with three more layers of dough, using eight sheets for each layer, brushing each sheet with butter and sprinkling each layer with one-fourth of the pecan mixture. Cover with the remaining eight sheets of phyllo dough, brushing each sheet with butter. Cut diagonally into 1-inch diamond shapes, cutting through all the layers. Bake for 35 to 40 minutes or until brown. Remove from the oven. Pour the honey mixture over the warm baklava. Let stand for 1 hour or longer before serving. Serve chilled or at room temperature.

Yield: 24 pieces

GREEK HONEY CAKES

The traditional Greek treat is only enhanced by using pure Florida honey.
Serve with iced tea for a delightful afternoon indulgence.

HONEY SYRUP	$1/4$ teaspoon salt
1 cup honey	$1/2$ teaspoon cinnamon
$1/2$ cup sugar	$1/8$ teaspoon nutmeg
$3/4$ cup water	$3/4$ cup ($1 1/2$ sticks) butter, softened
1 teaspoon lemon juice	$3/4$ cup sugar
	3 eggs
CAKE	$1/4$ cup milk
1 cup all-purpose flour	$1/2$ teaspoon grated orange zest
$1 1/2$ teaspoons baking powder	1 cup chopped walnuts

For the syrup, bring the honey, sugar and water to a boil in a saucepan. Reduce the heat and simmer for 5 minutes. Skim the foam. Add the lemon juice. Simmer for 2 minutes. Remove from the heat to cool.

For the cake, preheat the oven to 350 degrees. Mix the flour, baking powder, salt, cinnamon and nutmeg together. Beat the butter and sugar in a bowl until light and fluffy. Add the eggs one at a time, beating well after each addition. Add the flour mixture and mix well. Stir in the milk. Fold in the orange zest and walnuts. Spoon into a greased and floured 9×13-inch cake pan. Bake for 30 minutes. Cool in the pan. Pour the syrup over the top of the cake. Cut diagonally into sixteen 2-inch diamond shapes.

Yield: 16 servings

FLORIDA HONEY

Where you find oranges, orange blossom honey will surely be

nearby. When the orange blossoms perfume the air, the bees are

hard at work, and the result is a delicate and fragrant honey.

The rarest Florida honey is Tupelo honey. With a mild flavor and

heavy body, its special composition keeps it from ever granulating.

BERN'S CARROT CAKE BROWNIES WITH TOASTED PECAN FROSTING

*Based on the famous King Midas dessert served in the Harry Waugh Dessert Room at
Bern's Steak House, this portable version was created by Bern's chefs
for Super Bowl XLIII, held in Tampa in 2009. Executive Pastry Chef Kim Yelvington
added a toasted pecan frosting just for us.*

BROWNIES
1 1/2 cups all-purpose flour
1 teaspoon cinnamon
1/2 teaspoon nutmeg
Dash of salt
1/2 cup (1 stick) unsalted
butter, softened
1 1/4 cups sugar
2 eggs
5 tablespoons buttermilk
1 teaspoon vanilla extract
1/4 teaspoon peach schnapps

1/4 cup pecans, toasted and
finely chopped
3 carrots, peeled and shredded
(about 1 3/4 cups)

TOASTED PECAN FROSTING
1/2 cup (1 stick) unsalted butter,
softened
12 ounces cream cheese, softened
3/4 cup confectioners' sugar
1/4 cup pecans, toasted

For the brownies, preheat the oven to 350 degrees. Sift the flour, cinnamon, nutmeg and salt together. Beat the butter and sugar at low speed in the bowl of a stand mixer fitted with the paddle attachment until smooth. Beat at medium speed until light and fluffy. Add the eggs, buttermilk, vanilla and schnapps a small amount at a time, beating well after each addition and stopping to scrape down the side of the bowl occasionally. Add the flour mixture and mix well. Scrape down the side of the bowl. Stir in the pecans and carrots. Spoon into a buttered 9×13-inch baking pan. Bake for 20 to 30 minutes or until the edges pull from the side of the pan. Remove from the oven to cool.

For the frosting, beat the butter in the bowl of a stand mixer fitted with the paddle attachment until soft and creamy. Add the cream cheese and beat until smooth. Beat in the confectioners' sugar. Fold in the pecans with a spatula. Spread over the cool brownies.

Yield: 24 servings

BLUEBERRY CRUMBLE CHEESECAKE BARS

*A hint of lemon gives these delectable cheesecake bars a
fresh flavor. Perfect for a crowd.*

2 cups all-purpose flour	16 ounces cream cheese, softened
1/2 cup packed light brown sugar	1/2 cup granulated sugar
1 cup (2 sticks) butter	2 eggs
1 cup fresh or frozen blueberries	1 teaspoon vanilla extract
3 tablespoons water	1 cup all-purpose flour
1/4 cup granulated sugar	1 cup packed light brown sugar
2 teaspoons fresh lemon juice	1/2 cup quick-cooking oats
1 cup fresh or frozen blueberries	1/2 cup (1 stick) butter, softened

Preheat the oven to 350 degrees. Mix 2 cups flour and 1/2 cup brown sugar in a medium bowl. Cut in 1 cup butter with a pastry blender until crumbly. Press evenly in a 9×13-inch baking pan lined with foil. Bake for 15 minutes or until light brown.

Combine 1 cup blueberries, the water, 1/4 cup granulated sugar and the lemon juice in a small saucepan and mix well. Cook over medium heat for 10 minutes. Add 1 cup blueberries. Cook for 8 minutes, stirring frequently. Keep warm.

Beat the cream cheese and 1/2 cup granulated sugar at medium speed in a mixing bowl until smooth. Add the eggs one at a time, beating well after each addition. Beat in the vanilla. Pour over the warm crust. Spoon the blueberry mixture evenly over the cream cheese mixture. Mix 1 cup flour, 1 cup brown sugar, the oats and 1/2 cup butter in a bowl until crumbly. Sprinkle over the blueberry layer. Bake for 30 to 35 minutes or until the filling is set. Cut into bars. Serve warm or cold.

Yield: 24 servings

MINI PEANUT BUTTER AND CHOCOLATE TARTS

These tarts find a scrumptious balance of salty and sweet flavors. They fit right in with the casual ambiance of so many Tampa get-togethers.

TART SHELLS
1 1/4 cups all-purpose flour
3/4 teaspoon baking soda
1/2 teaspoon salt
1/2 cup (1 stick) butter, softened
1/2 cup creamy peanut butter
1/2 cup granulated sugar
1/2 cup light brown sugar
1 egg
1/2 teaspoon vanilla extract

CHOCOLATE FILLING
1 cup (6 ounces) milk chocolate chips
1 cup (6 ounces) semisweet
    chocolate chips
1 (14-ounce) can sweetened
    condensed milk
1 teaspoon vanilla extract

For the tart shells, preheat the oven to 325 degrees. Sift the flour, baking soda and salt together. Beat the butter, peanut butter, granulated sugar and brown sugar in a large mixing bowl until smooth and creamy. Add the egg and vanilla and mix well. Stir in the flour mixture. Shape the dough into forty-eight 1-inch balls. Place each ball in a miniature muffin cup. Bake for 15 minutes. Remove from the oven and immediately make indentations in the center of each using the back of a spoon. Cool in the pan. Remove to a wire rack.

For the filling, melt the chocolate chips in a heavy saucepan over low heat, stirring constantly. Stir in the condensed milk and vanilla. Spoon into a pastry bag or a sealable plastic bag with a corner removed. Pipe the filling into the tart shells. Let stand until the filling hardens before serving.

Yield: 4 dozen

PEPPERMINT CHOCOLATE CHIP CHEESECAKE BITES

These miniature cheesecakes are an irresistible bite-size treat.

8 chocolate graham cracker rectangles,
crushed (1/3 package)
1/4 cup sugar
1/4 cup (1/2 stick) butter, melted
6 peppermint candies
8 ounces cream cheese, softened
1/4 cup sugar
2 tablespoons all-purpose flour

1 egg
1 cup sour cream
1/4 cup miniature semisweet
chocolate chips
1/2 teaspoon peppermint extract
1/2 cup whipped topping
6 peppermint candies, crushed
2 tablespoons chocolate sprinkles

Preheat the oven to 325 degrees. Mix the graham cracker crumbs, 1/4 cup sugar and the butter in a bowl. Press a heaping teaspoon of the crumb mixture in the bottom of each miniature muffin cup coated with nonstick cooking spray. Bake for 5 minutes. Process 6 candies, the cream cheese, 1/4 cup sugar, the flour, egg and sour cream in a food processor until smooth. Stir in the chocolate chips and peppermint extract. Pour in the prepared crusts. Bake for 15 minutes or until small cracks form on the tops. Cool in the pan on a wire rack for 30 minutes. Remove from the pan and cool completely. Top each cheesecake with 1 teaspoon of the whipped topping. Sprinkle with the crushed candies and chocolate sprinkles.

Yield: 2 dozen

CHOCOLATE-DIPPED STRAWBERRIES

Melt 8 ounces of milk, dark or white chocolate with 1/4 teaspoon vegetable oil in a double boiler or a heatproof bowl set over simmering water. Wash and dry 12 large, ripe strawberries. Dip the point of each strawberry in the melted chocolate to coat. Place on baking parchment to cool. Serve at room temperature or slightly chilled for a luscious but light after-dinner treat.

CHOCOLATE LOVERS' CUPCAKES

Who doesn't love a cupcake? Easy preparation and a luscious
homemade frosting make these extra special.

CUPCAKES
1 (2-layer) package chocolate fudge
cake mix
1 1/2 cups (9 ounces) miniature
chocolate chips
1 teaspoon vanilla extract
1 (4-ounce) package chocolate
cook-and-serve pudding mix
1 envelope whipped topping mix

CHOCOLATE FROSTING
1 cup (2 sticks) unsalted butter,
softened
6 cups confectioners' sugar
1 1/4 cups unsweetened baking cocoa
1/2 cup milk
2 teaspoons vanilla extract

For the cupcakes, preheat the oven to 350 degrees. Toss 1/4 cup of the dry cake mix with the chocolate chips in a small bowl to coat and set aside. Prepare the remaining cake mix using the package directions. Add the vanilla and pudding mix and beat for 1 minute. Add the whipped topping mix. Beat at medium speed until the batter is light and fluffy. Fold in the chocolate chips. Fill lined muffin cups a little over three-fourths full. Bake for 20 to 25 minutes or until a knife inserted into the centers comes out clean. For a cake, spoon the batter into three 9-inch cake pans and bake for 25 to 28 minutes or until a knife inserted into the centers comes out clean. Cool on a wire rack.

For the frosting, beat the butter, 4 cups of the confectioners' sugar, the baking cocoa, 1/4 cup of the milk and the vanilla at low speed in a mixing bowl for 1 minute. Beat at medium speed for 4 minutes. Add the remaining 2 cups confectioners' sugar 1 cup at a time, beating for 2 minutes after each addition. Add the remaining 1/4 cup milk or additional confectioners' sugar if needed for the desired consistency. Spread over the cupcakes. You made add additional baking cocoa to taste. The frosting may be stored in an airtight container at room temperature for several days. For vanilla frosting, substitute an additional 1 teaspoon vanilla extract for the baking cocoa. Use clear vanilla extract for a bright white frosting.

Yield: 18 cupcakes

TRIPLE CHOCOLATE COOKIES

*The ultimate chocoholics dream—an inspirational blend of
chocolate, chocolate, and more chocolate!*

4 ounces unsweetened chocolate
$1/2$ cup (3 ounces) chocolate chips
3 cups all-purpose flour
1 teaspoon baking soda
$1/2$ teaspoon baking powder
1 teaspoon coarse salt
1 cup (2 sticks) butter, softened

1 cup granulated sugar
1 cup packed light brown sugar
2 eggs
1 teaspoon vanilla extract
6 ounces white chocolate, chopped
6 ounces semisweet chocolate, chopped

Preheat the oven to 325 degrees. Melt the unsweetened chocolate and chocolate chips in a small heatproof bowl over simmering water, stirring frequently. Remove from the heat to cool. Whisk the flour, baking soda, baking powder and salt in a medium bowl. Beat the butter, granulated sugar and brown sugar in a large mixing bowl for 2 minutes or until light and fluffy. Add the eggs and beat well. Beat in the vanilla and melted chocolate. Add the flour mixture and mix well. Fold in the white chocolate and chocolate chips.

Drop by $1/4$ cupfuls 2 inches apart onto a cookie sheet sprayed with nonstick cooking spray or lined with baking parchment. Bake for 15 to 18 minutes or until the tops appear slightly dry and just until the centers of the cookies are set. Cool on a wire rack for 10 minutes. Remove to a wire rack to cool completely. You may chill the dough for several hours before baking to help prevent the dough from spreading too much while baking. The baking time may need to be adjusted.

Yield: about 2 dozen

RICOTTA CHEESE COOKIES

*Ideal on a dessert platter, these traditional Italian cookies are like
eating pillows of sweet, creamy goodness.*

COOKIES
2 cups all-purpose flour
1/2 teaspoon baking soda
1/2 teaspoon salt
1 cup (2 sticks) butter, softened
1/2 cup soft ricotta cheese
1 cup sugar
1 teaspoon vanilla extract

1 egg, beaten
Sprinkles (optional)

SIMPLE ICING
1 cup confectioners' sugar
1 to 2 tablespoons boiling water
Anise, lemon or orange extract to taste

For the cookies, preheat the oven to 325 degrees. Sift the flour, baking soda and salt together. Beat the butter and cheese in a mixing bowl until smooth and creamy. Add the sugar and beat until light and fluffy. Add the vanilla and mix well. Add the egg and mix well. Add the flour mixture gradually, beating constantly. Drop by teaspoonfuls onto a cookie sheet lined with baking parchment. Sprinkle the tops with sprinkles. Bake for 7 to 9 minutes or until the cookies have a matte finish. The cookies will not be light brown or brown on the bottom. Cool on the cookie sheet for 5 to 10 minutes or until cool to the touch.

For the icing, sift the confectioners' sugar into a bowl. Add the boiling water 1 tablespoon at a time until the desired consistency, stirring constantly. Stir in flavoring. For the assembly, dip the cookies in the icing or spread over the tops with an offset spatula. Store in a well sealed container.

Yield: about 4 dozen

LEMON LIME SHORTBREAD

*Specks of lemon and lime zest infuse this dough with a light citrus flavor. Make the dough
ahead of time and freeze it to have on hand for unexpected guests.*

1/2 cup granulated sugar
1 1/2 teaspoons lemon zest
1 1/2 teaspoons lime zest
1 cup (2 sticks) unsalted
butter, softened
1/4 cup confectioners' sugar, sifted

1/2 teaspoon sea salt
2 egg yolks, at room temperature
2 cups all-purpose flour
1 egg yolk, at room temperature
Sparkling sugar

Mix the granulated sugar, lemon zest and lime zest in a small bowl. Beat the butter at medium
speed in a bowl until smooth and creamy. Add the zested granulated sugar, confectioners' sugar and salt
and beat for 1 minute or until smooth. Beat in 2 egg yolks one at a time. Add the flour and beat at low
speed just until blended. Divide the dough into two equal portions. Shape each portion into a smooth
log the diameter of a half dollar. Wrap each log well in plastic wrap. Chill for 2 hours to 3 days or freeze
for up to 6 weeks. Preheat the oven to 350 degrees. Unwrap one of the logs. Brush with egg yolk and
coat with sparkling sugar. Cut into 1/3- to 1/2-inch slices. Place on a greased cookie sheet. Bake for
10 minutes or until the edges are golden brown. Cool on the cookie sheet for 1 to 2 minutes. Remove
to a wire rack to cool completely. Repeat with the remaining log.

Yield: 3 dozen

COOKING WITH LEMONS

*Lemons are like liquid sunshine. They bring out the flavor
in foods and make everything taste brighter and fresher. Lemon trees,
both the common Eureka and Lisbon varieties and sweeter, thin-
skinned Meyer lemons, are found in backyards across our area, so
this refreshing citrus fruit is always close at hand.*

FRESH ORANGE SHERBET

*Squeezing fresh orange juice for this sherbet will perfume your kitchen
with the scent of Florida orange groves.*

1 cup sugar	1 tablespoon fresh lemon juice
1 1/2 tablespoons orange zest	1 teaspoon vanilla extract
2 cups fresh orange juice	1 1/2 cups milk

Combine the sugar, orange zest, orange juice, lemon juice and vanilla in a large bowl and stir until the sugar is completely dissolved. Stir in the milk. Chill for 1 hour. Pour into an ice cream freezer container. Freeze using the manufacturer's directions.

Yield: 6 servings

CREAMY LEMON MINT SORBET

*This tangy lemon sorbet is equally delightful when substituted with lime.
Be warned—it is sweet and tart, and a small scoop goes a long way.*

1 cup fat-free Greek yogurt	1/2 cup water
3/4 cup sugar	1/4 cup fresh lemon juice
1/2 cup Mint Simple Syrup (page 28)	1 1/2 teaspoons lemon zest

Process the yogurt, sugar, Mint Simple Syrup, water, lemon juice and lemon zest in a blender until well blended. Pour into an ice cream freezer container. Freeze using the manufacturer's directions. Substitute lime for the lemon in this recipe. Use the same amount of juice and omit the zest. Add a drop of green food coloring, if desired.

Yield: 8 servings

MENUS FROM THE JUNIOR LEAGUE OF TAMPA CULINARY COLLECTION

BAYSIDE BRUNCH

Zesty Sunday Morning Bloody Mary (CTC)

Pineapple Tea (LOP)

Mushroom Fritatta (STS)

Paradise Salad (CTC)

Bacon Swiss Tarts (STS)

Blueberry Banana Bread (EDF)

TAKE ALONG TAILGATE

Sippin' Sangria (STS)

Roasted Bar Nuts (EDF)

Florida Avocado Salsa (CTC)

Tailgate Roast Beef on Rolls (LOP)

Shrimp Pasta Salad (CTC)

Florida Orange Cookies (EDF)

DINNER IN A BREEZE

Mango Pineapple Punch (CTC)

Garlic Cheese Spread (EDF)

Guava Glazed Pork Tenderloin (CTC)

Corn Soufflé (LOP)

Strawberry Spinach Salad (STS)

Chocolate Fudge Sauce *over ice cream* (EDF)

CATCH OF THE DAY

Mojito (LOP)

Brie and Apricot Phyllo Bites (EDF)

Gazpacho with Shrimp (CTC)

Planked Seatrout (CTC)

Black Bean and Jasmine Rice Salad (LOP)

Coconut Cream Pie (STS)

THE FLORIDA PANTRY

Florida's balmy weather has many obvious benefits, one of the most significant being our plentiful produce. Our local harvest and the influences of our distinct ethnic cuisines set the Florida pantry apart. Keep these ingredients on hand to make your cooking come alive!

Aromatics—Ginger, garlic, and onion pair up well with citrus and tropical fruit flavors. These ingredients are so common it's hard to cook without them!

Avocado—The Florida avocado, or alligator pear, is larger and milder than Haas or other California varieties. It has less fat per ounce than a Haas, but may be used interchangeably. With a thin, glossy green skin, it is ripe when it yields to gentle pressure.

Berries—Strawberries and blueberries are two of our most important cash crops. Plant City is known as the "Winter Strawberry Capital of the World," as berries are ready to be harvested and enjoyed as early as December.

Cheeses—Florida is home to almost 140 dairy farms. Feta, ricotta, Swiss, Parmesan, and mascarpone are just a few of the cheeses featured in Tampa Bay area cuisines.

Chorizo sausage—Originally from the Iberian Peninsula, chorizo is a dry, cured, pork sausage seasoned with paprika and garlic. The red color and robust flavor come from the introduction of pimento, which was added when the Spaniards returned from the New World. Today chorizo is included in many savory Latin dishes from soups to paella.

Citrus Fruits—Citrus is Florida's number one crop. Second only to Brazil in orange production, our grapefruit harvest is the largest in the world. The ruby red grapefruit is native to Florida, and other citrus fruits such as lime, Key lime (see entry), lemon, tangerine, pomelo, tangelo, and kumquat are grown here.

Fish & Shellfish—Shrimp, clams, bay scallops, oysters, blue and stone crabs, grouper, seatrout, flounder, pompano, snapper, mullet, and Spanish mackerel are some of our most important commercial aquaculture harvests. Snook and redfish are found in the mangroves and grassy flats of Tampa area waters.

Fresh Herbs—Basil, cilantro, dill weed, mint, parsley, sage, rosemary, and thyme are all grown commercially in Florida. Several more choices are available for the home garden, including oregano, which is widely used in Latin cuisine. A good rule of thumb when substituting fresh herbs for dry is to use one tablespoon of fresh herbs for every specified teaspoon of dry herbs.

Guava—This delicate tree fruit is eaten fresh, in paste form, canned, or as a jelly. For a classic pairing, serve fresh guava or guava paste with cream cheese as a light dessert, or in a pastry for breakfast.

Honey—All honey produced in Florida must be 100% pure, and labeled as such. The most commonly found Florida honey flavors are the orange blossom, clover, and wild flower.

Key lime—A small citrus fruit typically found in the Florida Keys, Key limes also grow well in Tampa Bay area backyards. The skin is leathery to the touch, and the sweet acidic flesh is yellow. As Key limes ripen, their color changes from green to yellow, and the acid level falls. A true Floridian knows that authentic Key lime pie is yellow, not green.

Melons—Synonymous with summer, watermelon production occurs in Florida from April to July. Icebox watermelons, so-called for their small size, and seedless watermelons are increasingly common, making it easier than ever to enjoy this sweet treat. Cantaloupe, which is more accurately known as muskmelon, is a spring melon available from Florida farms from mid-March to June.

Nuts—Native to the Mississippi basin, pecans are grown commercially in North Florida, but can be found in backyards throughout our area. Other local favorites include pine nuts in Italian dishes and walnuts in Greek recipes.

Peppers—Bell peppers are an important crop in the Sunshine State. Many other varieties, including ancho, cayenne, cherry, cubanelle, Hungarian wax, jalapeño, sweet frying, and serrano, are also well suited to Florida's climate and featured in regional and ethnic cuisines.

Tropical fruits—Locally grown banana, mango, lychee, passion fruit, papaya, and many more exotic species can be found in backyards and at farmers' markets.

Squashes—Summer squashes such as yellow crookneck, straightneck, and zucchini are widely grown in fall, winter, and spring. Ironically, the only time of year they are not grown is the middle of the summer, when it is too hot!

Tomatoes—Florida is the main domestic source for all fresh, field-grown tomatoes sold in U.S. markets from October through June. The soil in Ruskin, twenty-five miles from Tampa, is particularly well suited for growing many varieties of tomatoes. The Ruskin Tomato Festival has celebrated the harvest since 1935.

Tubers—New and fingerling potatoes are grown in Florida during the winter and spring. Their skin can be white or red, as well as Yukon gold or blue. Sweet potatoes are a particular favorite of area cooks.

RECIPE CONTRIBUTORS AND TESTERS

A special thank you to all of The Junior League of Tampa members, families, and friends who submitted their treasured recipes for consideration. We also recognize with deep appreciation our many testers who opened their kitchens and gave us invaluable feedback.

Pamela Adler
Lisa Andrews
Nicole Andriso
Alexa Argerious
Kate Gainey Asturias
Andrea Augustine
Amy Ayres
Catie Baker
Jodi Bakshi
Elizabeth Baldwin
Joanne Baldy
Kimberly Barrs
Beth Benn
Carol Bennett
Weatherly Bentley
Megan Berrigan
Emery Bettis
Charlene Bleakley
Natalie Boe
Lynda Boyet
Shannon Brannagan
Jane Brannan
Patricia Brawley
Jaime Brewer
Sarah Bricklemyer
Jana Bridge
Wendy Brill
Susan Brindise
Sarah Brooks
Alyssa Brownell
Laurie Buckey

Natalie Bugg
Caroline Burt
Campbell Burton
Laurie Ann Burton
Lindsey Butler
Julie Byrd
Allison Campbell
Paula Cardoso
Casey Carefoot
Ashley Carl
Jen Carlstedt
Lindsay Carter
Kelly Catoe
Donna Christian
Jen Cisneros
Taylor Clifton
Tracy Clouser
Rachel Coleman
Mary Ellen Collins
Shannon Coram
Patti Cowart
Kate Crawford
Colleen Crosby
Chloe Cullinan
Renee Dabbs
Tina Dampf
Ginny Daniel
Aadonia de la Torre
Danielle Dennis
Kealoha Deutsch
Pam Divers

Terrie Dodson
Gretchen Dominguez
Tracie Domino
Nicole Dorr
Lindsay Dorrance
Connie Duglin
Erin Eckhouse
Debby Edwards
Katie Einselen
Vicki Elsberry
Sara Evans
Robyn Fedorovich
Louise Ferguson
Joanna Finks
Kathy Fitzhugh
Lynn Footlick
Bethany Fox
Katherine Frazier
Lori Friesz
Laura Frost
Lisa Gabler
Suzanne Gabler
Zoe Gallina
Rebecca Jo Garbrick
Melissa Garvey
Melissa Gelwix
Carmen Gibson
Stephanie Gibson
Pat Gillen
Nicole Gitney
Laura Lee Glass

Anna Glover
Susan Goldberg
Nicole Gomez
Betsy Graham
Jen Granger
Kristi Grooms
Jan Gruetzmacher
Paola Gruner
Erin Hall
Judy Hall
Kimberly Hannah
Erica Hanson
Sally Hardee
Sarane Harrell
Sarah Hart
Susan Hawkins
Lynne Hildreth
Sally Hill
Laura Hobby
Lori Hoffman
Michelle Hogan
Marissa Holdorf
Carolyn Holman
Karin Hotchkiss
Tara Hoss
Bridgette Howell
Jenn Hunt
Sue Isbell
Ann Marie Iwanicki
Ellen James
Krisden Jernigan

Beth Johnson
Katie Johnson
Aspen Kahl
Beth Kalicki
Leigh Kaney
Kristin Kiser
Diana Klingensmith
Sarah Kodadek
Loralee Koontz
Veronica Kruchten
Elizabeth Kurz
Malloy Lacktman
Georgia Laliotis
Trish Lane
Susan Lang
Kimberly LaPorte
Catherine Larkin
Andrea Layne
Jenifer LeBeau
Sherry Leffers
Ruth Levant
Valarie Lewis
Brita Wilkins Lincoln
Lee Lowry
Fe Luttrell
Ashley Macaluso
Heather Mackin
Winifer MacKinnon
Susan Major
Christine Malpartida
Michele Mangan
Christa Mannhart
Michelle Marvel
Rebecca Burton Martin
Caro Massari
Christina Matassini
Marysue Mathews

Karen May
Heather McKean
Carroll McLain
Stephanie McNeil
Lauren McQueen
Carla Megerian
Susan Mendelson
Christina Merrild
Lisa Metheny
Angier Miller
Jenn Millman
Stephanie Minter
Cammie Monroe
Mindy Murphy
Kelly Nelson
Laura Nies
Jovanna Nogues
Kate Novinskie
Lisa Nugent
Kelly O'Brien
Carolyn Orr
Kimberly Osborne
Brandi Ottinger
Jenifer Ownby
Sandra Palmer
Laurie Parker
Lauren Patterson
Sarah Perron
Anne Person
Aly Peterson
Cindy Wells Peterson
Chris Phillips
Carolyn Piper
Harriet Plyler
Anita Popp
Jennifer Pressley
Kathleen Purdy

Katherine Raser
Denise Rasmussen
Angie Ratliff
Becky Rauenhorst
Kimberly Muller Reed
Brandi Reeves
Alison Reteneller
Clara Reynolds
Mary Riding
Layla Ringhoff
Jodi Rivera
Christina Roberts
Lori Root
Mary Kay Ross
Meghan Ross
Franci Rudolph
Ashley Rushing
Lynette Russell
Carla Saavedra
Kristie Salzer
Laura Sansone
Krystal Schofield
Jessica Shea
Melissa Shelton
Jennifer Simpson-Oliver
Dorimar Siviero-Minardi
Mary Ann Skinner
Julia Smith
Kelly Smith
Robyn Stambaugh
Jennifer Stauffer
Susan Steele
Sarah Stichter
Jennifer St. Jacques
Maggie Storino
Steely Taglione
Jacqueline Taylor

Barbara Tesar
Kathleen Thaxton
Michelle Thomas
Susan Thompson
Dawn Tiffin
Suzanne Tow
Heather Trkovsky
Mary Lynn Ulrey
Lisl Unterholzner
Sarah Valentine
Eliot Van Dyke
Pat Van Dyke
Heather Vermette
Ginny Vickers
Margaret Vickers
Caroline Vostrejs
Stacey Waters
Elizabeth Watson
Laura Webb
Angela Weck
Gwen Weeks
Heather Werry
Julie Whitworth
Stephanie Wiendl
Tiffany Williams
Kimberly Williamson
India Witte
Mary Louise Wojahn
Laura Woodward
Leah Wooten
Christina Yeager
Laura York
Lori Youmans
Heidi Young
Kathryn Zahn
Aly Zamore
Susan Zelenka

INDEX

CAPTURE *the* COAST

The Junior League of Tampa, Inc.
87 Columbia Drive • Tampa, Florida 33606
813-254-1734 • cookbook@jlthq.com
www.jltampa.org

YOUR ORDER	QUANTITY	TOTAL
Capture the Coast at $21.95 per book		$
Savor the Seasons at $21.95 per book		$
EveryDay Feasts at $21.95 per book		$
The Life of the Party at $21.95 per book		$
JLT Culinary Collection at $60.00 (includes *The Life of the Party, EveryDay Feasts, Savor the Seasons* and *Capture the Coast*)		$
The Gasparilla Cookbook at $14.95 per book		$
Tampa Treasures at $19.95 per book		$
Shipping and handling at $4.95 for one book; $2.00 for each additional book		$
	Subtotal	$
Florida residents add 7% sales tax		$
	TOTAL	$

Name

Address

City   State   Zip

Telephone

Method of Payment: [ ] VISA   [ ] MasterCard
                       [ ] Check payable to The Junior League of Tampa

Account Number   Expiration Date

Signature

Photocopies will be accepted.